Grammar Expert

Series Editors:
Sarah Bideleux
Gill Mackie

THOMSON

HEINLE

Australia   •   Canada   •   Mexico   •   Singapore   •   United Kingdom   •   United States

Grammar Expert 3
Series Editors: Sarah Bideleux, Gill Mackie

Publisher: *Carl Wantenaar*
Director of Content Development: *Anita Raducanu*
International Marketing Manager: *Ian Martin*
Production Project Manager: *Natasa Arsenidou*
Print Buyer: *Marybeth Hennebury*
Compositor: *Vasiliki Christoforides*

Project Manager: *Diane Flanel Piniaris*
Contributing Writers: *Rachel Finnie, Nicholas Stephens*
Consulting Editor: *James W. Brown*
Illustrators: *Ilias Sounas*
Cover/Text Designer: *Sophia Fourtouni, Natasa Arsenidou*
Printer: *CTPS*

Cover Image: www.photos.com

For permission to use material from this text
or product, submit a request online at
http://www.thomsonrights.com

Any additional questions about permissions
can be submitted by email to
thomsonrights@thomson.com

ISBN-13: 978-960-403-290-7
ISBN-10: 960-403-290-9

Printed in China
1 2 3 4 5 6 7 8 9 10   10 09 08 07

For more information, contact Thomson Heinle,
25 Thomson Place, Boston, Massachusetts 02210 USA,
or you can visit our Internet site at elt.thomson.com

Contents

OH, DON'T WORRY. HE'S SHOUTING NOW, BUT SOMETIMES HE GETS REALLY ANGRY.

Simple Present

Affirmative
I/you walk
he/she/it walks
we/you/they walk

Negative
I/you do not (don't) walk
he/she/it does not (doesn't) walk
we/you/they do not (don't) walk

Question
Do I/you walk?
Does he/she/it walk?
Do we/you/they walk?

Short Answers

Yes, I/you do.   No, I/you don't.
Yes, he/she/it does.   No, he/she/it doesn't.
Yes, we/you/they do.   No, we/you/they don't.

We use the Simple Present:

➤ to talk about habits.
She walks the dog every morning.
They don't stay out late on Sundays.

➤ to talk about things that are true in general.
It snows heavily in Canada in the winter.
Dogs like bones.

➤ to talk about permanent states.
He works in a bank.
Do you live in an apartment?

➤ for sports commentaries.
Mike heads for the basket and shoots – 2 points!

---

1   Complete the sentences with the Simple Present.

Ex.   *They ....go............... skiing in December. (go)*

1   We ....walk........ to work every morning. (walk)

2   Mom .....not call..... her friend in California every week. (not call)

3   Water ....boil......... at 100 degrees Celsius. (boil)

4   The goalkeeper ....dive......... to his right and ....make......... a great save! (dive, make)

5   Some birds ....fly......... to warmer countries in the winter. (fly)

6   Dad ....watch....... a lot of baseball on TV in the summer. (watch)

7   I ....study....... English in the evening. (study)

8   Our neighbor .....not plays.... his music until midnight every night. (not play)

9   She ....not helps...... her mother with the housework every day. (not help)

10   I ....write....... e-mails every day. (write)

2 ▸ **Write questions.**

Ex. *Dad sings in the shower.*
Does Dad sing in the shower?

1 Your friend speaks to his cousin in French.
Do your friend speak to his cousin in French ?

2 Scientists work on new ideas every day.
Does Scientists work on new ideas every day ?

3 Ronaldo scores a goal every time he plays soccer.
Does Ronaldo scores a goal every time he play soccer ?

4 My brothers own a large house in Atlanta.
Do your brother own a large house in Atlanta ?

5 He replies to all his e-mails immediately.
Does he reply to all his e-mails immediately ?

Adverbs of Frequency with the Simple Present

never	hardly ever	rarely/seldom	sometimes	often/usually	always
0% ←				→	100%

Adverbs of frequency come before the main verb but after the verb *to be*.
I often eat eggs for breakfast.
She's seldom at home on Friday evenings.

3 ▸ **Rewrite the sentences with the adverbs of frequency in the correct place.**

Ex. *He plays tennis on Friday evening. (often)*
He often plays tennis on Friday evening.

1 I watch TV until midnight on Mondays. (rarely)
I rarely

2 It is very hot in New York in November. (never)
It is never hot

3 Do you travel to Boston? (sometimes)
Do you travel to Boston sometimes

4 We invite lots of people to our parties. (usually)
We usually invite lots of people

5 My wife drinks coffee in the evening. (seldom)
My wife seldom drinks

6 I listen to classical music. (hardly ever)
I hardly ever listen to classical

Time Expressions with the Simple Present

every day	in December
every week	in the morning/afternoon/evening
every month	on Monday morning/on Mondays
every year	at 7 o'clock/at noon/at night
every summer	three times a day
every other day	once a week
every two months	twice a month

Time expressions usually come at the end of the sentence. We put them at the beginning of the sentence when we want to emphasize them.
He goes to the gym every other day.
In March we always visit our friends in London.

4 ▶ Write answers that are true about yourself.

Ex. *What do you do on Saturdays?*
On Saturdays I go to the park with my friends.

1 Where do you go on Saturdays?
I go to church on Saturday

2 What do you do twice a day?
I brust my teeth

3 Who do you see every week?
I see alot of customer

4 Who do you talk to every morning?
I talk to customer every morning

5 Which newspaper do you read on Sundays?
I read sunday Globe

6 Do you usually take a vacation in August?
Sometime not all the time

Present Continuous

Affirmative
I am (I'm) talking
you are (you're) talking
he/she/it is (he's/she's/it's) talking
we/you/they are (we're/you're/they're) talking

Negative
I am not (I'm not) talking
you are not (aren't) talking
he/she/it is not (isn't) talking
we/you/they are not (aren't) talking

Question
Am I talking?
Are you talking?
Is he/she/it talking?
Are we/you/they talking?

Short Answers

Yes, I am. | No, I'm not.
Yes, you are. | No, you aren't.
Yes, he/she/it is. | No, he/she/it isn't.
Yes, we/you/they are. | No, we/you/they aren't.

We use the Present Continuous to talk about:

➤ actions in progress at the time of speaking.
I'm eating my lunch at the moment.
She is working at her desk right now.

➤ actions in progress around the time of speaking.
Her friend's working in Japan this month.
They're living with their cousin for two months.

➤ changes that are happening gradually.
The hole in the ozone layer is getting bigger all the time.

5 ▶ Complete the sentences with the verbs from the box. Use the Present Continuous.

chase   get   land   make   not work   repair   rest   stay   write

Ex. I ......*am writing*...... an e-mail to my friend at the moment.

1 Look! The plane ...*is landing*... now!
2 She ...*is making*... lunch in the kitchen.
3 The climate ...*is getting*... warmer.
4 That dog ...*is chasing*... a cat up the tree!
5 This week my boss ...*is staying*... at a resort in the Caribbean.
6 Our manager ...*is not working*... out of town this week.
7 The technicians ...*is repairing*... my computer at the moment.
8 Quiet! The children ...*is resting*... upstairs.

6 ▶ **Find the mistakes and rewrite the sentences correctly.**

Ex. *We aren't watch TV at the moment.*
..........*We aren't watching TV at the moment.*..........

1 Are he reading his new book in the living room?
Is
....

2 Annie picking is flowers in the garden.
..........*is picking*..........................

3 Why you aren't eating your dinner?
..........*aren't you*..........................

4 I'm to learning Spanish this summer.
....

5 How they are traveling to work this week?
..........*are*................................

6 We aren't listen to the radio.
........................*listening*..........

Time Expressions with the Present Continuous

at the moment	this week
for the time being	this month
now	this year
right now	today
this morning/afternoon	these days

7 ▶ **Choose the correct answer.**

Ex. *I always* (eat) / *am eating eggs for breakfast.*

1 Where *do you go* / *are you going* right now?
2 This morning she *is doing* / *does* the laundry.
3 I *am surfing* / *surf* the Internet twice a day.
4 Who *is he speaking* / *does he speak* to on the phone now?
5 They *are staying* / *stay* with their friends for the time being.
6 Every July we *are going* / *go* to our cabin in the mountains.
7 *Do you have* / *Are you having* a birthday party every year?
8 Where *do you usually play* / *are you usually playing* chess?
9 My brother *is swimming* / *swims* in a competition today.
10 Our dog always *is listening* / *listens* to everything we say!

Stative Verbs

We don't usually use stative verbs in the Present Continuous. Stative verbs are:

➤ verbs connected with our senses:
feel, hear, see, smell, sound, taste
These flowers smell lovely.

➤ verbs that express emotions:
dislike, hate, like, love, need, prefer, want
He loves Indian food.

➤ verbs that express understanding or opinion:
appear, believe, forget, hope, imagine, know, mean, realize, remember, seem, think, understand, wonder
She seems to be very good at her job.

➤ verbs that express possession:
belong to, have, own, possess
That black dog belongs to us.

Some stative verbs are used in the Present Continuous, but with a change in meaning:

➤ feel, have, look, see, think
I feel I have upset you. (I sense this.)
I am feeling the bump on my head. (I am touching it.)

We have a lot of CDs. (We own them.)
He is having lunch now. (He is eating lunch now.)

You look sad. (You appear to be sad.)
I'm looking at the children playing in the park.
(I'm watching them.)

We see a deer in the forest every evening. (We look at it.)
I'm seeing the dentist today. (I have an appointment.)

She thinks English grammar is easy. (She believes this.)
He is thinking of taking a vacation. (He is considering it.)

Notes

We can also use *I see* when we want to show we understand something.
"I can't eat peanuts because I'm allergic to them." "I see."

8 ▶ **Choose the correct answer.**

Ex.   *I am not believing /* ⟨*don't believe*⟩ *you!*

1   I *love / am loving* listening to rock music.

2   *Is he seeing / Does he see* the doctor right now?

3   I never *am forgetting / forget* my wife's birthday.

4   He *thinks / is thinking* of going to Hawaii.

5   I *understand / am understanding* everything you are saying.

6   These potatoes *taste / are tasting* wonderful!

7   How many cars *does he own / is he owning*?

8   They *have / are having* lunch right now.

9   What *are you doing / do you do* at the moment?

10   Why *are you looking / do you look* at me like that?

9 ▶ **Complete the e-mail with the Simple Present or the Present Continuous.**

🖂 e-mail

| Send Now | Send Later | Save as Draft | Add Attachments | Signature ▾ | Options ▾ | Rewrap |

From: ▾
To:
Cc:
Bcc:
Subject:
▷ Attachments: *none*

Default Font ▾ Text Size ▾ | **B** *I* U T | ≡ ≡ ≡ | ≔ ≔ ≔ ≔ | **A** ▾ ▾ | —

Hi, Jane,

I (Ex.) ....*think*............ (think) it's my turn to write, so here's my message!

I (1) ....*hope*......... (hope) you (2) ...*are*....*having*.... (have) a nice day today. What (3) .... you .... (do)? I (4) ....*am*......... (be) busy at the moment because I (5) ....*m writing*.... (write) a report for work. It always (6) ...*take*........... (take) me ages! I usually (7) ....*make*........ (make) notes first, but not today. I (8) ...*m trying*.... (try) to finish it quickly because we have a meeting tomorrow morning.

At the moment my roommate (9) .....*is making*..... (make) dinner in the kitchen. I (10) .... (imagine) she (11) ....*is cooking*........ (cook) chicken. We always (12) ....*have*.......... (have) chicken on Wednesdays. I (13) ....*think*........ (think) she (14) ...*is calling*...... (call) me because the food is ready. I'll write again tomorrow.

Love,
Katie

10 ▶ **Find the extra word in each sentence and write it on the dotted line.**

Ex.   *What are you do doing this weekend?* ....*do*...........

1   We does hope the boss is pleased with our work. .....*does*....

2   I am usually wash my hair twice a week. ....*am*......

3   Why is the nurse be examining that boy's arm? ....*be*......

4   How often he does David go to the gym? ....*he*......

5   Are they be watching TV in the living room now? ....*be*......

6   What are do you think of the new neighbors? ......*are*......

7   He does plays football very well. ....*does*......

8   Aren't you going reading your new book at the moment? ...*going*....

9   Do I hear a strange noise outside. ......*Do*........

10   Where do they to live? ....*to*......

11 ▶ **Check (✓) the correct sentence.**

Ex. *Do you thinking about going to Hawaii?* _____
Are you thinking about going to Hawaii? _✓_

1 Are you using new computer programs this year? _____
Do you use new computer programs this year? _✓_

2 Ken always is washing his car on Sundays. _____
Ken always washes his car on Sundays. _✓_

3 We don't like swimming in very cold water. _✓_
We aren't liking swimming in very cold water. _____

4 Why is he owning two houses? _____
Why does he own two houses? _✓_

5 I know this isn't my pen. _✓_
I am knowing this isn't my pen. _____

6 She rarely surfs the Internet. _✓_
She is rarely surfing the Internet. _____

7 I'm not believing anything he says. _____
I don't believe anything he says. _✓_

8 He hardly ever discusses work with any of his friends. _✓_
He is hardly ever discussing work with any of his friends. _____

Pairwork

Work with a partner.

➤ Tell each other things you usually do and things you never do.
➤ Talk about what you are and are not doing at the moment. Think of as many things as you can!
For example:
I'm speaking to you.
I'm sitting on a hard chair.
I'm not learning French.
I'm not writing a letter.

Writing

Write an e-mail to a friend. Talk about what you're doing at the moment and what you usually do on Saturday and Sunday. Ask your friend some questions, too.

| e-mail |
Send Now Send Later Save as Draft Add Attachments Signature ▼ Options ▼ Rewrap
From:
To:
Cc:
Bcc:
Subject:
Attachments: *none*
Default Font ▼ Text Size ▼ B *I* U T

Present Perfect & Present Perfect Continuous

Present Perfect

Affirmative

I/you have (I've/you've) gone
he/she/it has (he's/she's/it's) gone
we/you/they have (we've/you've/they've) gone

Negative

I/you have not (haven't) gone
he/she/it has not (hasn't) gone
we/you/they have not (haven't) gone

Question

Have I/you gone?
Has he/she/it gone?
Have we/you/they gone?

Short Answers

Yes, I/you have.   No, I/you haven't.
Yes, he/she/it has.   No, he/she/it hasn't.
Yes, we/you/they have.   No, we/you/they haven't.

We use the Present Perfect:

➤ to talk about something that happened in the past, but it is not important when.
She has broken her arm.
Have you visited many foreign countries?

➤ to talk about something that happened in the past that has an effect on the present.
She has broken her arm, so she can't play basketball.
They haven't eaten with chopsticks before, so they don't know how to use them.

➤ to talk about something that began in the past and is still going on.
I've been an art student for two years.
He's lived in Boston since 2005.

➤ to talk about something that has just happened. (Note: In American English, we can also express this with the Simple Past.)
They've just arrived. = They just arrived.

➤ after superlatives.
He's the nicest man I've ever met.
This is the best movie we've ever seen.

---

1 ▸ **Complete the sentences with the Present Perfect.**

Ex. I .....*have eaten*..... *too much chicken, so I won't have dessert. (eat)*

1   My business partner ......*has gone*...... to Boston for a week. (go)

2   ......*Has he read*...... the book I gave him? (he / read)

3   I ...*have not eaten*... all day. I'm starving! (not eat)

4   They ....*have finish*.... all their work. (finish)

5   She ...*has send*... five e-mails today. (send)

6   They ...*have never been*... to Mexico before. (never / be)

7   ......*Have they live*...... in the same house for thirty years? (they / live)

8   I ...*haven't forgot*... to bring my reading glasses today. (not forget)

Thinkaboutit

The Present Perfect Simple is formed with **have/has** and the past participle of the main verb. See page 162 for a list of irregular verbs.

2 ► Write answers using the words in parentheses.

Ex. *Have you ever lived in Los Angeles? (San Diego)*
    No, we haven't. We've lived in San Diego.

1 Has he been a teacher for ten years? (five years)
   No, he hasn't. He has been a teacher for five years.

2 Have they been to Rome and Venice? (Florence and Pisa)
   ....

3 Have you known your friend for very long? (a few months)
   ....

4 Has he sent her a letter? (e-mail)
   ....

5 Has it snowed this month? (rain)
   ....

Time Expressions with the Present Perfect

already	since 1999	once
ever	since the summer	twice
for	since June	three times
for a long time/for ages	so far	always
just	until now	before
never	yet	how long

3 ► Choose the correct answer.

Ex. *Have you .... seen a hurricane?*
    (a) *ever*   **b** *never*   **c** *once*

1 He has .... cleaned the car.
   a yet   **b** ever   **c** already

2 I haven't seen them .... Saturday.
   a once   **b** since   **c** until

3 Have you repaired the TV ....?
   a just   **b** yet   **c** so far

4 Hurry! The tennis match has .... started!
   a just   **b** since   **c** yet

5 They've .... been to Africa.
   a ever   **b** once   **c** never

6 I've read five Agatha Christie mysteries ....
   a so far   **b** for   **c** yet

7 They haven't seen each other ....
   a never   **b** for ages   **c** three times

8 I've eaten rice .... this week.
   a never   **b** so far   **c** twice

Have Been and Have Gone

We use *have been* to say that someone has gone to a place and has come back.
I've only been to Paris once.
Have you ever been to China?

We use *have gone* to say that someone has gone to a place and has not returned yet.
My parents have gone to Florida.

We also use *have gone* with phrases with *go + gerund.*
Have you ever gone skiing?

4 ► **Check (✓) the correct sentence.**

Ex. *He has gone to work and he'll be home at six.* ✓
    He has been to work and he'll be home at six. ____

1   We have gone to London twice in the past three years. ____
    We have been to London twice in the past three years. ____

2   Have you ever gone to Washington, D.C.? ____
    Have you ever been to Washington, D.C.? ____

3   My friends have gone to China. They left Tuesday. ____
    My friends have been to China. They left Tuesday. ____

4   Carlos has been in Brazil all summer, but now he's home. ____
    Carlos has gone in Brazil all summer, but now he's home. ____

5   "Where's Alison?" "She's been to the library." ____
    "Where's Alison?" "She's gone to the library." ____

6   Have you ever been to Egypt? ____
    Have you ever gone to Egypt? ____

7   I was worried. Where have you gone? ____
    I was worried. Where have you been? ____

8   Everybody has gone to the movies. I'm all alone. ____
    Everybody has been to the movies. I'm all alone. ____

Present Perfect Continuous

Affirmative
I/you have (I've/you've) been working
he/she/it has (he's/she's/it's) been working
we/you/they have (we've/you've/they've) been working

Negative
I/you have not (haven't) been working
he/she/it has not (hasn't) been working
we/you/they have not (haven't) been working

Question
Have I/you been working?
Has he/she/it been working?
Have we/you/they been working?

Short Answers

Yes, I/you have.   No, I/you haven't.
Yes, he/she/it has.   No, he/she/it hasn't.
Yes, we/you/they have.   No, we/you/they haven't.

We use the Present Perfect Continuous to talk about:

➤ something that started in the past and has continued until now or that started and has happened repeatedly until now.
We've been living in this house for nine years.
He's been making model trains since he was ten years old.

➤ something that happened repeatedly or continuously in the past that has visible results in the present.
Your hands are filthy! Have you been fixing your car again?
He's been playing soccer in the rain, and now he's covered in mud.

5 **Complete the sentences with the Present Perfect Continuous.**

Ex. They ......*have been swimming*...... for two hours. (swim)

1 I .... this book all morning. (read)

2 She .... e-mails for the last hour. (not write)

3 We .... English for very long. (not study)

4 We .... the movie with our friends. (discuss)

5 They .... food for the party all day. (prepare)

6 I .... to this CD for half an hour. (listen)

7 The dogs .... all night! (bark)

8 I .... well lately. (not feel)

9 His English .... steadily since last year. (improve)

10 She .... Her eyes are all red. (cry)

> **Thinkaboutit**
>
> The Present Perfect Continuous is formed with **have/has** + **been** + verb + **-ing**.

6 **Complete the questions with the Present Perfect Continuous and write answers.**

Ex. *Has the sun been shining*.............................. all day? (the sun / shine) **X**
    No, it hasn't.........................

1 .... in the lake? (he / swim) ✓

   ....

2 .... on the chair? (the cat / sleep) **X**

   ....

3 .... hard lately? (you / work) ✓

   ....

4 .... the piano all afternoon? (she / play) **X**

   ....

5 .... in front of the TV all day? (they / sit) ✓

   ....

6 .... all night? (he / travel) **X**

   ....

Time Expressions with the Present Perfect Continuous

all day/night
for a long time
for (very) long
for years
lately
recently
since

7 ▶ **Choose the correct answer.**

Ex. *She's been waiting* for / (since) *1 o'clock.*

1   They have been listening to rock music for *hours / all night.*

2   Have you been working on this project for *a long time / all the time?*

3   We've been studying for a test *all morning / in the morning.*

4   The baby has been sleeping peacefully *all night / for recently.*

5   I've been driving a car since *years / I was eighteen.*

6   My friend has been trying to lose weight *all day / recently.*

7   Have those boys been playing football *all the afternoon / all afternoon?*

8   She hasn't been feeling well *since / for* a few days.

9   We have been moving furniture *all day / this day.*

10   I think you've been working too hard *lately / since weeks.*

Present Perfect or Present Perfect Continuous?

We use the Present Perfect:

➤ to talk about something we have done or achieved. The action is complete.
I've written twelve e-mails today.
He's passed his driving test.

➤ for quantity, to answer the question *how much/many?* or *how many times?*
I've eaten six bananas today!
He's drunk a bottle of milk.

We use the Present Perfect Continuous:

➤ for duration, to talk about something that has lasted for a long time. It doesn't matter whether the action is complete or not.
She's been typing all afternoon.
They've been watching TV all morning.

➤ to talk about *how long?*
(How long has he been working here?) *He's been working here for eighteen months.*

Notes

Sometimes we can use either form with no change in meaning. This is true especially for sentences with *for* and *since* that talk about very long-lasting habits or repeated activities that began in the past and continue into the present.

Habit
He's lived here for years. = He's been living here for years.

Repeated Activity
He's come here for years. = He's been coming here for years.

8 ▶ **Complete the sentences with the Present Perfect or the Present Perfect Continuous.**

Ex. *It ....has been snowing.......... all night. (snow)*

1   Look at your hands! .... on the car again? (you / work)

2   I .... half the report. (already / write)

3   .... any good documentaries lately? (you / see)

4   How long .... today? She looks like she's ready to fall asleep! (she / study)

5   What .... all afternoon? (you / do)

6   I .... the housework yet. (not finish)

7   Oh no! The computer .... (crash)

8   He .... all night. He's exhausted now. (travel)

9   .... any new clothes this week? (you / buy)

10   How many times .... to contact him? (you / try)

9 > Complete the passage with the Present Perfect or the Present Perfect Continuous.

The doctors and nurses at the hospital (Ex.) ......*have been working*...... (work) very hard lately. Many children (1) .... (have) high fevers and their parents (2) .... (take) them to the hospital. For the past two weeks, doctors (3) .... (tell) parents what to do, and experts on TV (4) .... (give) worried parents advice. Fortunately, fewer children (5) .... (become) ill in the last few days, and many of those who were unwell (6) .... (recover). They (7) .... (feel) much better since their temperatures went down and some (8) .... (go) back to school. Doctors say they (9) .... (treat) over 2,000 children in the past month, but they (10) .... (see) only twenty sick children this week. It looks like the epidemic is finally under control.

10 > Choose the correct answer.

Ex. .... *his latest movie yet?*

    (a) *Have you seen*   **b** *Have you been seeing*   **c** *Have you see*

1   My father .... his own car since he was nineteen years old.
    a has owned   **b** has been owning   **c** owns

2   Those children .... chocolate all day!
    a has been eating   **b** have eaten   **c** have been eating

3   We haven't been to the movies .... a few weeks.
    a since   **b** yet   **c** for

4   I'm tired because I .... for the last hour.
    a have jogged   **b** have jogging   **c** have been jogging

5   He .... to learn how to drive for ages.
    a has been trying   **b** has tried   **c** has been tried

6   They've .... had lunch, so they're not hungry now.
    a yet   **b** just   **c** only

7   The bus .... arrived yet, so we'll be late for work.
    a haven't   **b** hasn't   **c** has

8   I .... ten jackets today and I can't decide which I like best.
    a have tried on   **b** haven't tried on   **c** have been trying on

11 > Find the mistakes and write the sentences correctly.

Ex. *They haven't been listened to the radio.*
    They haven't been listening to the radio....................

1   We've already seeing the new movie.
    ....

2   What have you been done all day?
    ....

3   Have you been hearing that Jim is married now?
    ....

4   He isn't here right now; he's yet left.
    ....

5   I haven't been knowing Lily for very long.
    ....

6   Have you been finishing all the work yet?
    ....

12 ▶ **Answer the questions in your own words.**

Ex. *What have you eaten today?*
     I've eaten a bowl of cereal, a salad and an apple....

1   What have you been doing all day?

     ....

2   What books or magazines have you read recently?

     ....

3   How long have you been living at your current address?

     ....

4   How many CDs have you bought in the last two months?

     ....

5   What have you been doing for the last 30 minutes?

     ....

Pairwork

Work with a partner. Take turns. Ask and answer the following questions:

➤ What new things have you learned this year?
➤ What interesting places have you visited since you were ten years old?
➤ What have you been thinking about for the last hour?
➤ What have your friends been doing all day today?

Writing

1 Write a short paragraph about all the things that you have done this week at home and at work or school.

2 Write a short paragraph about what has been happening in your life, your country or the world this year.

OH, YOU'RE NEW! DON'T WORRY. YOU'LL GET USED TO THE COFFEE HERE.

Simple Past – Regular Verbs

Affirmative	Negative	Question
I/you looked	I/you did not (didn't) look	Did I/you look?
he/she/it looked	he/she/it did not (didn't) look	Did he/she/it look?
we/you/they looked	we/you/they did not (didn't) look	Did we/you/they look?

Short Answers

Yes, I/you did.	No, I/you didn't.
Yes, he/she/it did.	No, he/she/it didn't.
Yes, we/you/they did.	No, we/you/they didn't.

Simple Past – Irregular Verbs

Affirmative	Negative	Question
I/you saw	I/you did not (didn't) see	Did I/you see?
he/she/it saw	he/she/it did not (didn't) see	Did he/she/it see?
we/you/they saw	we/you/they did not (didn't) see	Did we/you/they see?

Short Answers

Yes, I/you did.	No, I/you didn't.
Yes, he/she/it did.	No, he/she/it didn't.
Yes, we/you/they did.	No, we/you/they didn't.

We use the Simple Past to talk about:

➤ actions that started and finished in the past.
I lost my wallet yesterday. She didn't sleep well last night.

➤ actions that happened one after the other in the past.
He woke up, got out of bed and took a shower. I put on my coat, picked up my bag and left the house.

➤ actions that were repeated or were habits in the past.
Her grandfather made wooden toys. Did they have CDs in the year 1960?

See the Irregular Verbs list on page 162.

Time Expressions with the Simple Past

a week ago	last summer
a month ago	last year
a year ago	on Saturday
in January	on August 4th
in 1999	the day before yesterday
in my youth	the other day
last night	when I was five years old
last week	yesterday

Time expressions usually come at the beginning or the end of a sentence.

3

1 ▶ **Today is October 13th. Read and write about what Leo did and didn't do yesterday.**

My Diary
October 12th

repair my bicycle ✓
write ten e-mails ✓
study English ✓
find my glasses ✓
fix the table ✗
make my bed ✓
do the dishes ✗
sell my old videos ✗
get a new notebook ✓
sleep all afternoon ✗
take my suit to the cleaner's ✓

Ex. *He repaired his bicycle.*
1 ....
2 ....
3 ....
4 ....
5 ....
6 ....
7 ....
8 ....
9 ....
10 ....

2 ▶ **Write answers using the words in parentheses.**

Ex. *Did you go to the theater last night? (restaurant)*
   No, I didn't. I went to a restaurant.

1 Did they have fish for dinner? (soup and salad)
   ....

2 Did you buy a new computer? (DVD player)
   ....

3 Did they break the kitchen window? (bedroom window)
   ....

4 Did Sarah pay for the tickets? (John)
   ....

5 Did he forget his coat? (umbrella)
   ....

6 Did she take a photograph of you? (the view)
   ....

Simple Past or Present Perfect?

We use the Simple Past to describe actions that happened at a specific time in the past, a series of actions in the past and past habits (actions that we usually did in the past but don't do now).
She took her final exams the day before yesterday.
They walked to the museum, looked at the exhibition and had lunch at a restaurant nearby.
They played basketball when they were young.

We use the Present Perfect to describe completed past actions that have an effect on the present, actions that happened in the past, but when they happened is not important, and actions that started in the past but are still going on now.
He has seen that DVD so he doesn't want to see it again.
They've had that car for nine years.

Notes
When we talk about someone who is no longer alive, we use the Simple Past to describe what they did.
When we talk about someone who is still alive, we use the Present Perfect to talk about what they have done.
Beethoven composed great symphonies. (He's no longer alive and cannot compose any more.)
Ronaldo has scored some great goals. (He's still alive and will score some more.)

3 Use the prompts in each row to write sentences with the pattern: *A week ago ... , but since then ... .*

A week ago	Since then
I / ill	doctor / give me / some medicine
my cat / lost	it / come / home
we / on vacation	we / return / home
the car / dirty	I / wash / it
she / not know / the city	she / seen / lots of sights
the students / buy / new books	they / read / them all

Ex. *A week ago I was ill, but since then the doctor has given me some medicine.*

1 ....

2 ....

3 ....

4 ....

5 ....

4 Complete the sentences with the Simple Past or the Present Perfect.

Ex. We ....*have already drunk*............ all the water we ....*brought*.......... with us. (already drink, bring)

1 I .... your brother last week, but I .... his wife yet. (see, not meet)

2 He .... his bed already, but he .... his room yet. (make, not clean)

3 Last night I .... a DVD at my friend's house and we .... a pizza. (watch, order)

4 .... you .... Harry long or .... you only just ....
friends? (know, become)

5 They .... to Brazil for three months and .... home. (go, recently arrive)

6 She .... animals all her life, so she .... delighted when she got a job at the vet's. (like, be)

7 Charles Dickens .... many books and a lot of them are still popular. (write)

8 Michael .... with us last night because he .... well all week. (not come, not be)

Past Continuous

Affirmative

I was dancing
you were dancing
he/she/it was dancing
we/you/they were dancing

Negative

I was not (wasn't) dancing
you were not (weren't) dancing
he/she/it was not (wasn't) dancing
we/you/they were not (weren't) dancing

Question

Was I dancing?
Were you dancing?
Was he/she/it dancing?
Were we/you/they dancing?

Short Answers

Yes, I was.	No, I wasn't.
Yes, you were.	No, you weren't.
Yes, he/she/it was.	No, he/she/it wasn't.
Yes, we/you/they were.	No, we/you/they weren't.

We use the Past Continuous to talk about:

➤ actions that were in progress at a specific time in the past.
I was watching a movie at 10:30 last night.
They were waiting for the bus when I saw them.

➤ two or more actions that were in progress at the same time in the past.
My sister was making lunch while I was washing my hair.
The dogs were barking and the people were shouting.

➤ background events in a story.
The wind was whistling through the trees and the thunder was crashing all around us.
The children were playing happily and their parents were talking.

➤ an action in progress in the past that was interrupted by another.
She was cooking dinner when a police officer rang the doorbell.
They were waiting for Bob when they saw the accident.

3

Time Expressions with the Past Continuous

all day yesterday
all evening
at 10 o'clock last night
as/while
last Sunday
last year
this morning

---

5 ▷ Complete the sentences with the verbs from the box. Use the Past Continuous.

| bark | not work | read | set | sleep | take | talk |

Ex. *The neighbors' dogs* ....*were barking*........ *all night. I didn't sleep a wink!*

1   Which book .... you .... yesterday evening?

2   Brian was home yesterday because he ....

3   Who .... your secretary .... to on the phone a minute ago?

4   At 2 o'clock this morning I ....

5   All the students .... a test this morning.

6   I .... the table and my cousin was cooking dinner.

---

6 ▷ Fill in the blanks with the Simple Past or the Past Continuous.

Ex. *While I* ....*was living*........ *in Paris, I* ....*went*........ *to a French school. (live, go)*

1   When the snow ...., my friends and I .... for the bus. (start, wait)

2   When we .... young, we .... in Texas. (be, live)

3   While our boss .... the problem, Mark .... (explain, daydream)

4   .... you .... long hair when you .... twelve years old? (have, be)

5   .... you .... to music while you ....? (listen, work)

6   I .... you because I .... about my vacation. (not hear, think)

7   I .... down my book, then I .... the light off and .... to sleep.
    (put, turn, go)

8   The students .... attention while the teacher .... to them. (not pay, read)

Used To

Affirmative

I/you used to work
he/she/it used to work
we/you/they used to work

Negative

I/you did not (didn't) use to work
he/she/it did not (didn't) use to work
we/you/they did not (didn't) use to work

Question

Did I/you use to work?
Did he/she/it use to work?
Did we/you/they use to work?

Short Answers

Yes, I/you did.   No, I/you didn't.
Yes, he/she/it did.   No, he/she/it didn't.
Yes, we/you/they did.   No, we/you/they didn't.

We use *used to* for actions that we did regularly in the past but that we don't do now. We also use it for states that existed in the past but that don't exist now.
My parents used to go dancing every Saturday night, but they don't now.
I didn't use to like her, but now I do.

---

7 ▸ **Complete the sentences with the correct form of used to and the verb in parentheses.**

Ex. I ......*didn't use to study*........ English as a child, but I do now. (not study)

1 Those people .... next door to us a few

   years ago. (live)

2 .... in a hotel when you went to Florida?

   (you / stay)

3 We .... a dog, but we've got two now! (not have)

4 Young people .... computers like they do

   nowadays. (not use)

5 My parents .... a beach house on Long Island every summer. (rent)

6 .... as much money in the old days as they do now? (people / have)

7 He .... us English until last year. (teach)

8 My cat .... as friendly as it is now. (not be)

9 That house .... different when my grandparents lived there. (look)

10 I .... as hard as I do now. (not work)

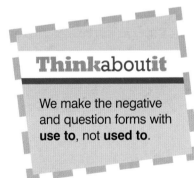

Thinkabout**it**

We make the negative and question forms with **use to**, not **used to**.

Be Used To

Affirmative
I am used to working
you are used to working
he/she/it is used to working
we/you/they are used to working

Negative
I am (I'm) not used to working
you are not (aren't) used to working
he/she it is not (isn't) used to working
we/you/they are not (aren't) used to working

Question
Am I used to working?
Are you used to working?
Is he/she/it used to working?
Are we/you/they used to working?

Short Answers

Yes, I am.	No, I'm not.
Yes, you are.	No, you aren't.
Yes, he/she/it is.	No, he/she/it isn't.
Yes, we/you/they are.	No, we/you/they aren't.

Be used to is followed by a gerund (verb + *-ing*) or by a noun.
He's used to living in a big city.
We're tourists. We're not used to the customs here.

We use *be used to* to talk about things that are no longer unusual or new. We can use it to talk about the present, past or future.
She is used to getting up early in the morning now.
They weren't used to studying alone until they went to college.
Today solar and wind power are not very common. In the future, people will be used to using these forms of energy.

Notes

Remember: With *be used to*, we make the negative and question forms with *used to*.

---

8 ▶ **Complete the sentences with the correct form of be used to.**

Ex.   *He was born in the country. He ......isn't used to...... living in a big city.*

1   They come from Alaska so they .... cold weather.
2   I have just started a new job so I .... the new routine yet.
3   Alan has just bought a laptop but he .... working with it yet.
4   We .... traveling every day because we don't live near the office.
5   .... you .... wearing a uniform to work?
6   I'm learning Spanish but I .... speaking it all the time.
7   We live near the railway line so we .... hearing trains going past.
8   He's a policeman so he .... asking people questions.

Get Used To

Affirmative
I/you get used to working
he/she/it gets used to working
we/you/they get used to working

Negative
I/you do not (don't) get used to working
he/she/it does not (doesn't) get used to working
we/you/they do not (don't) get used to working

Question
Do I/you get used to working?
Does he/she/it get used to working?
Do we/you/they get used to working?

Short Answers

Yes, I/you do.	No, I/you don't.
Yes, he/she/it does.	No, he/she/it doesn't.
Yes, we/you/they do.	No, we/you/they don't.

Get used to is followed by a gerund (verb + *-ing*) or by a noun.
He's slowly getting used to being here.
We got used to our new professor quite quickly.

We use *get used to* to talk about new situations that are still strange but that are becoming more familiar than they were at first. We can use it to talk about the present, past or future.
They are getting used to living in the city.
She hasn't got used to speaking Spanish yet.
Will we ever get used to this?

Notes

Remember: We make the negative and question form with *used to*.

9 > Find the mistakes and write the sentences correctly.

Ex. *I am get used to reading newspapers in English.*
    I am getting used to reading newspapers in English.

1 He can't got used to seeing so many cars.
....

2 It's difficult to get used to live in a new house.
....

3 At first the traffic kept him awake all night, but he slowly get use to it.
....

4 They haven't get used to working at home.
....

5 Have you got use to being the only woman in the office?
....

6 He quickly get use to walking to work.
....

10 > Choose the correct answer.

Ex. *He .... used to using the computer now.*
    a *is got*   **b** *gets*   **c** *is getting*

1 Years ago people .... travel everywhere by car.
  a get used to   **b** didn't use to   **c** were use to

2 Young people .... working with computers.
  a used to   **b** get use to   **c** are used to

3 She soon .... sharing an apartment with her friends.
  a is used to   **b** got used to   **c** was use to

4 When I was a baby, I .... cry a lot.
  a use to   **b** get used to   **c** used to

5 They .... riding their bikes to work.
  a used to   **b** got use to   **c** are used to

6 I can't .... living in a cold climate.
  a get used to   **b** be used to   **c** am used to

7 .... people staring at you because your hair is so long?
  a Got you used to   **b** Are you used to   **c** Did you use to

8 We .... used to living in our new house.
  a be   **b** are getting   **c** get

Pairwork

Work with a partner. Take turns. Ask and answer questions about:

➤ things you have never done but want to do.
➤ things you did and really enjoyed.
➤ things you did but hated.
➤ places you have never visited but want to go to.

Writing

Write a short paragraph about yourself. Talk about things you used to do when you were young, things you are (not) used to doing nowadays, and things you are still getting used to or have got used to during the last two years.

....
....
....
....
....
....
....
....
....

4 Past Perfect & Past Perfect Continuous

I HAD JUST DECIDED TO QUIT, BUT THEN I GOT MY TELEPHONE BILL.

Past Perfect

Affirmative
I/you had (I'd/you'd) finished
he/she/it had (he'd/she'd/it'd) finished
we/you/they had (we'd/you'd/they'd) finished

Negative
I/you had not (hadn't) finished
he/she/it had not (hadn't) finished
we/you/they had not (hadn't) finished

Question
Had I/you finished?
Had he/she/it finished?
Had we/you/they finished?

Short Answers

Yes, I/you had.	No, I/you hadn't.
Yes, he/she/it had.	No, he/she/it hadn't.
Yes, we/you/they had.	No, we/you/they hadn't.

We use the Past Perfect to talk about:

➤ something that happened in the past before another action in the past. For the action that happened first, we use the Past Perfect. For the action that happened second, we use the Simple Past.
The fire had gone out before the firefighters got there.

➤ something that happened before a specific time in the past.
They had all left by midnight.

➤ something that happened in the past and had an effect on a following action or state.
He had forgotten his wallet, so he borrowed some money from me.

See the Irregular Verbs list on page 162.

Time Expressions with the Past Perfect

after	just	
already	by (a time or date)	never ... before
as soon as	when	

He had already finished the report by Monday afternoon.
She had just sat down when the phone rang.
They had never been to Mexico before.

1 ▶ Complete the sentences with the Past Perfect.

Ex. They ......*had never run*...... a marathon before. *(never run)*

1 I felt sick after I .... three slices of cake. (eat)

2 My daughter did well on her finals because she .... a lot.
   (study)

3 We .... all the food before the guests arrived.
   (already prepare)

4 They .... their old house, so they had enough money to buy
   a bigger one. (sell)

5 He .... so far before, so he was very proud of himself. (never swim)

6 The patient's condition .... by Monday. (improve)

7 I .... the book by 7 o'clock. (finish)

8 The rain .... when we left for the park. (just stop)

9 He .... when we got there. (already leave)

10 She was upset because she .... all her exams. (fail)

> **Thinkaboutit**
>
> We make the Past Perfect with **had** + past participle.

2 ▶ Write questions and negative sentences.

Ex. *The movie had started by 10 o'clock.*

Had the movie started by 10 o'clock?

The movie hadn't started by 10 o'clock.

1 They'd eaten all the bread before the waiter brought our food.

   ....

   ....

2 He had owned that car for twelve years when he sold it.

   ....

   ....

3 John had lost ten pounds when he stopped dieting.

   ....

   ....

4 Paul had just come home from work when the earthquake struck.

   ....

   ....

5 She went to the dentist after she had called him.

   ....

   ....

Past Perfect Continuous

Affirmative

I/you had (I'd/you'd) been sleeping
he/she/it had (he'd/she'd/it'd) been sleeping
we/you/they had (we'd/you'd/they'd) been sleeping

Negative

I/you had not (hadn't) been sleeping
he/she/it had not (hadn't) been sleeping
we/you/they had not (hadn't) been sleeping

Question

Had I/you been sleeping?
Had he/she/it been sleeping?
Had we/you/they been sleeping?

Short Answers

Yes, I/you had.   No, I/you hadn't.
Yes, he/she/it had.   No, he/she/it hadn't.
Yes, we/you/they had. No, we/you/they hadn't.

We use the Past Perfect Continuous to show that:

➤ one action in the past lasted a long time before another past action.
The baby had been crying for an hour before her mother came home.

➤ one action that lasted a long time in the past had an effect on a following action or state.
She had been training all morning, so she was exhausted when she got home.

---

3 ▶ **Complete the sentences with the Past Perfect Continuous.**

Ex. She ....*had been losing*........ weight for months before she found out she was ill. *(lose)*

1   We .... for hours before the theater opened. *(wait)*

2   My computer .... strangely all morning before it finally stopped working. *(behave)*

3   They .... for five hours before they finally took a break. *(study)*

4   The actors .... all morning so that the performance would be perfect. *(rehearse)*

5   She .... for thirty years before she decided to retire. *(teach)*

6   He .... for hours before he finally found his way out of the forest. *(walk)*

7   The snow .... all night, so everything was white when we woke up. *(fall)*

8   My brother .... stamps for years before he decided to change his hobby. *(collect)*

9   He .... a suit and tie to the office for years before he finally began to dress more casually. *(wear)*

10 Scientists .... for many years before they discovered a cure for the disease. *(work)*

Thinkabout**it**

We make the Past Perfect Continuous with **had been** + verb + **-ing**.

4 ▶ Write questions and answers using the Past Perfect Continuous.

Ex. *they / travel all night / when / they / reach the Canadian border (for four hours)*
Had they been traveling all night when they reached the Canadian border?
No, they hadn't. They had been traveling for four hours.

1 she / work here for a long time / before / she / lose her job (only a few weeks)

....

....

2 John / drive for hours / when / he / have the accident (twenty minutes)

....

....

3 they / live on campus for a year / before / they / get / an apartment (six months)

....

....

4 they / watch TV for ten minutes / before / I / get home (two hours)

....

....

5 the circus / travel for years / before / it / come to our town (a month)

....

....

Past Perfect or Past Perfect Continuous?

We can use both the Past Perfect and the Past Perfect Continuous to show that one action happened before another in the past.

We usually use the Past Perfect to talk about completed actions or a quantity of things completed.
He had finished writing all five e-mails, so he decided to take a break.

In contrast, we use the Past Perfect Continuous to emphasize the length of time an action lasted for. The action may or may not have been completed.
He had been painting the living room, so he was tired.

5 ▶ Choose the correct answer.

Ex. *The phone had been ringing / had rung ten times before he answered it.*

1 The thief *had stolen / had been stealing* cars for years before he was caught.

2 I was exhausted because I *had been painting / had painted* all day.

3 They *had been eating / had eaten* all the pizza before I got there.

4 We *had done / had been doing* the housework all day, so we decided to take a break.

5 The engine *had made / had been making* funny noises all week.

6 I couldn't believe it *had been snowing / had snowed* all night until I saw how white everything was.

7 Fortunately, the plane *had been landing / had landed* before the engine caught fire.

8 My father and his friend *had painted / had been painting* the entire house before Mom and I came home.

Past Perfect or Simple Past?

When we talk about two or more things that happened in the past, we use the Past Perfect to emphasize that one action had finished before another. We use the Simple Past to talk about the action that happened later.

He had already written his report before he took a break for lunch.
We were happy because we had all passed our exams.

6 ▸ **Choose the correct answer.**

Ex. *We .... the beds before our guests ....*
    ⓐ *had made, arrived*   **b** *made, had arrived*

1 They .... a great time before they .... the Caribbean.
    a had, had left   **b** had had, left

2 When I .... shopping, it .... raining.
    a had gone, had stopped   **b** went, had stopped

3 I .... his invitation before I .... the party was on the same day as yours.
    a accepted, had realized   **b** had accepted, realized

4 People .... to care about ecology after some animals .... extinct.
    a started, had become   **b** had started, became

5 Most of the tourists .... their lunch, so the guide .... them to get ready for the afternoon tour.
    a had finished, told   **b** finished, had told

6 He .... a lot of money when the police finally .... him.
    a had already stolen, arrested   **b** stole, had arrested

Past Perfect Continuous or Simple Past?

We use the Simple Past for actions that began and ended in the past. We use the Past Perfect Continuous for actions that were in progress in the past when, or before, another action happened.

We stayed in a hotel when we went to Ireland.
We had been traveling around Africa when Mara became ill.

7 ▸ **Complete the sentences with the Simple Past and the Past Perfect Continuous.**

Ex. We ......*had been waiting*...... for ages before he ......*arrived*...... at the Internet café. (wait, arrive)

1 The children .... exhausted because they .... basketball all afternoon. (be, play)

2 She .... for hours when the boss .... it was time to go home. (work, say)

3 The fans .... for half an hour before the rock star .... (wait, appear)

4 We .... the cat after we .... for him for two days. (find, look)

5 The magician .... for an hour before he .... one of his tricks right! (perform, get)

6 He .... ill, so he .... to see the doctor. (feel, decide)

8 ▶ **Complete the text with the Simple Past, Past Perfect or Past Perfect Continuous.**

My friends and I (Ex.) ....*had*................. (have) an interesting time last weekend. We all (1) .... (go) to stay in a cabin in the mountains because we (2) .... (think) about learning more about life in the country for a long time. We (3) .... (travel) for an hour when the car (4) .... (break down) and we had to walk the rest of the way!

When we (5) .... (reach) the cabin, we (6) .... (be) all very tired so we (7) .... (sleep) for an hour. Later on, we (8) .... (have) something to eat and (9) .... (start) exploring the area. We (10) .... (wander) around for about an hour when suddenly my friend (11) .... (find) some wild mushrooms. I (12) .... (read) books about wild mushrooms and so I (13) .... (know) it wasn't a good idea to eat them! When we (14) .... (collect) plants and flowers and (15) .... (take) photos for about two hours, we (16) .... (decide) we were hungry again, so we (17) .... (go) back to the cabin and made dinner. We (18) .... (eat) for only a few minutes when all the lights (19) .... (go out). Then we (20) .... (have) even more fun trying to find candles and light the fire in the dark! By the time we (21) .... (return) home, we (22) .... (learn) a lot about life in the country!

Pairwork

Work with a partner. Talk about:

➤ what you had done this morning before you left home.
➤ what your friends had been doing before you last saw them.
➤ what you had been doing before you went to bed last night.

Writing

Write a letter to your friend telling him/her about an exciting weekend you had recently. Talk about what you had been doing, what you had done and what you did. Use the tenses and the time expressions in this unit.

....
....
....
....
....
....
....
....
....
....
....
....
....

Review 1 (Units 1-4)

1 ▶ Complete the sentences with the Simple Present.

Ex. He ....*never borrows*........ his father's car. (never borrow)

1 .... to go the movies with us tonight? (you / want)

2 This .... the meal we ordered. (not be)

3 I .... about my friends from my old neighborhood. (often think)

4 We .... eggs for breakfast. (rarely eat)

5 How .... he .... to find enough time to do all his work? (manage)

6 He .... to drive into the city during rush hour. (not like)

7 He .... to call me, but he forgot yesterday. (usually remember)

8 Let's not buy those bananas. They .... ripe enough. (not look)

2 ▶ Complete the sentences with the verbs from the box. Use the Simple Present or Present Continuous.

belong	go	have	hate	hold	insist	meet	not understand	think (x2)

Ex. He ....*hates*.......... swimming in very cold water.

1 Why .... you .... your head? .... you .... a headache?

2 I .... we ought to make dinner now.

3 Who .... he .... after work every day?

4 How many times a week .... you usually .... to the gym?

5 Who .... that house .... to?

6 We .... your idea. Can you explain, please?

7 I .... on paying for lunch; you can pay next time.

8 He .... about quitting his job.

3 ▶ Find the mistakes and rewrite the sentences correctly.

Ex. *I go always shopping on Saturday morning.*
I always go shopping on Saturday morning.

1 Do she ever do anything except watch TV all day?

....

2 He plays tennis and meets friends on the evening.

....

3 For the time now I am living with my brother.

....

4 Last summer we are traveling around Scotland.

....

5 My cousin goes to Boston two a month.

....

6 What is he doing at the now?

....

7 We always are ready to learn about the environment.

....

8 I go to sleep rarely past midnight.

....

4 ▷ **Choose the correct answer.**

Ex. *She has worked /* (*has been working*) *in the new office all week.*

1   I *have thought / have been thinking* about applying for a job at the bank near my home.
2   Have you *been listening / listened* to the radio all this time?
3   You look as if you have *been running / run*; your face is all red!
4   We have *been changing / changed* the clocks, so it gets dark earlier now.
5   I can't believe you have *eaten / been eating* that whole pizza!
6   The dog has *barked / been barking* since 7 o'clock this morning.

5 ▷ **Complete the sentences with the Present Perfect or the Present Perfect Continuous.**

Ex. *They* ....*haven't decided*............ *on a date for the party yet. (not decide)*

1   She .... that novel for ten years, but she's still not done! (write)
2   I .... such spicy food before! (not taste)
3   We .... to call them all day, but no one answers the phone (try)
4   How long .... you .... to become a surgeon? (study)
5   That artist .... some amazing works of art. You can see them in the gallery downtown. (create)
6   .... you ever .... a complete change of career? (consider)
7   The birds .... making their nests. (start)
8   You .... a lot since I last saw you! (change)

6 ▷ **Rewrite the sentences with the words in parentheses in the correct place.**

Ex. *Have you been on vacation I last saw you? (since)*
   Have you been on vacation since I last saw you?
   ....

1   Has he had breakfast? (already)
   ....

2   Have you been living here? (how long)
   ....

3   She has left her friend's house. (just)
   ....

4   We haven't seen Pete a few days. (for)
   ....

5   Have you bought any clothes from this shop? (ever)
   ....

6   I haven't found anything interesting on the Internet. (so far)
   ....

7   The weather has been mild Saturday. (since)
   ....

8   The baby hasn't started to talk. (yet)
   ....

Review 1

7 Check (✓) the correct sentence.

Ex. *While I had been walking down the street, I saw two dogs.* ____
While I was walking down the street, I saw two dogs. ✓

1 My friend went to the dentist with me. ____
My friend was going to the dentist with me. ____

2 How did you manage while I was away? ____
How were you managing while I was away? ____

3 Were you finishing the report yet? ____
Have you finished the report yet? ____

4 Did you see your cousin last week? ____
Were you seeing your cousin last week? ____

5 How long did you have to wait for the bus? ____
How long were you having to wait for the bus? ____

6 While I was reading the paper, she was making breakfast. ____
While I am reading the paper, she was making breakfast. ____

8 Complete the sentences with the Simple Past or the Past Continuous.

Ex. *Yesterday we .... bought .... a new computer for my office. (buy)*

1 I .... when the alarm clock went off this morning. (sleep)
2 They .... about the free concert, so they .... it. (not know, miss)
3 Who .... you .... when you .... on the phone? (talk to, be)
4 They .... their way to my house very easily. (not find)
5 .... he .... to the children when you .... into the room? (talk, walk)
6 I .... last night when you .... (not read, call)
7 Who .... the living room window? (break)
8 She .... the house, ... the door and .... to the train station.
(leave, lock, walk)

9 Choose the correct answer.

Ex. *We .... in San Francisco, but now we live in Seattle.*
    a *use to live*   **b** *were living*   **ⓒ** *used to live*

1 Where did you .... to work before you started working here?
    a used   **b** use   **c** have

2 I can't .... being in charge of the office.
    a be used to   **b** get used to   **c** am used to

3 I didn't know you .... be a member of that club.
    a used to   **b** use to   **c** were

4 How often did it .... when you were little?
    a use to snow   **b** snowed   **c** used to

5 They .... a huge cake for the twins' birthday party.
    a used to buy   **b** bought   **c** use to buy

6 Did you .... jeans to school when you were younger?
    a use to wear   **b** were wearing   **c** use wear

7 They .... speaking Spanish when they lived in Mexico City.
    a used to   **b** were used to   **c** got used to

8 She .... living in a small apartment.
    a didn't used to   **b** used to   **c** isn't used to

10 Complete the sentences with the Past Perfect.

Ex. Astronauts ......*had walked*...... on the moon before I was born. (walk)

1 The tide .... out by the time we got to the beach (go)

2 .... he .... all his work before he went to the park? (do)

3 We .... painting by 10 o'clock. (finish)

4 I .... my medicine before I went to bed last night. (take)

5 Fortunately, she .... to go to the supermarket for me. (remember)

6 The chef .... enough sauce for the pasta. (not make)

7 .... she .... to you before she went out? (talk)

8 They .... to go to the beach, but their father took them anyway. (not ask)

11 Complete the sentences with the Past Perfect or the Past Perfect Continuous.
Use the verbs from the box.

| break down | disappear | go | listen | move | never be | not tell | tell | watch | water |

Ex. They .....*had been listening*..... to their CDs for hours.

1 She .... horror films all evening, so she went to sleep with the lights on.

2 He .... me exactly the same story the last time I saw him.

3 I couldn't drive to work because my car ....

4 He looked everywhere for the cats this morning, but they ....

5 He .... to New York for years, but he .... to the Statue of Liberty.

6 "Stuart doesn't live here anymore."

"I didn't know he ...."

7 We .... the garden for half an hour when it started to rain.

8 He .... anybody about his plans. How did you all find out?

12 Choose the correct answers.

Ex. *Nobody knew* what happened / had happened until they had seen / saw the 10 o'clock news.

1 Everybody *had / have* left the restaurant before the lights *have gone / went* out.

2 He *hadn't / didn't* realize he *had got / got* into the wrong car until he *was trying / tried* the key in the ignition!

3 After they *had been / had* working for five hours, their boss *has let / let* them have a coffee break.

4 He *has promised / has been promising* to fix that squeaking door for weeks, but he *hasn't done / didn't do* anything yet.

5 I *haven't understood / didn't understand* why she *was / was being* so scared of dogs until she told me she *had experienced / did experience* a nasty attack when she was a child.

6 I wonder if he *has / had* ever thought about asking his boss for a promotion. He *has been doing / has done* the same job for over ten years.

Future with Will

Affirmative
I/you will (I'll/you'll) go
he/she/it will (he'll/she'll/it'll) go
we/you/they will (we'll/you'll/they'll) go

Negative
I/you will not (won't) go
he/she/it will not (won't) go
we/you/they will not (won't) go

Question
Will I/you go?
Will he/she/it go?
Will we/you/they go?

Short Answers

Yes, I/you will.
Yes, he/she/it will.
Yes, we/you/they will.

No, I/you won't.
No, he/she/it won't.
No, we/you/they won't.

We use the Future with *Will*:

➤ for predictions.
He'll have a great time on vacation.
Will they succeed in their new business?

➤ for decisions made at the time of speaking.
I'm thirsty. I'll get some water.
I'll do that for you. I can see you're tired.

➤ for promises.
I'll be home before 10 o'clock.
I won't let you down.

➤ for threats.
Don't shout at me or I'll leave!
Stop complaining or I won't take you out again!

➤ for requests.
Will you come to the dentist with me, please?
Will you help me with my report?

➤ after some phrases, like *I expect, I'm sure, I wonder,* etc.
I'm sure you'll do well.
I wonder if he'll arrive on time?

Notes

Shall is a polite form of *will*. We sometimes use it with *I* or *we* in questions when we want to make an offer or suggest something.
Shall I bring you a pizza from from Luigi's?
Shall we go out on Saturday evening?

1 ▸ **Complete the sentences with the verbs from the box. Use the Future with Will.**

| buy | drive | enjoy | enter | get | learn | let | ~~live~~ | take | turn | work |

Ex.   *I'm sure you* ....*will live*......... *in a big city when you are older.*

1   They .... a lot about ancient Egypt on their tour of the Pyramids.

2   I'm cold. I think I .... the heating on.

3   Your boss .... really angry if you're late again!

4   I promise I .... you something nice for your birthday.

5   Do you think I .... the movie?

6   I wonder if John .... this competition and try to win a car!

7   This computer .... faster than your old one.

8   We .... into town later if it isn't raining.

9   I think I .... the dog for a walk now.

10 I .... you know as soon as the boss arrives.

2 ▸ **Write questions and negative sentences. Remember to use shall in questions that are offers or suggestions.**

Ex.   *They will get home late from work tomorrow.*
      Will they get home late from work tomorrow?
      They won't get home late from work tomorrow.

Thinkabout**it**

We usually use **won't** instead of **will not** in negative sentences.

1   Mr. Williams will interview all the job applicants.
    ....
    ....

2   The exhibition of modern art will be very interesting.
    ....
    ....

3   I'll make us a salad for lunch.
    ....
    ....

4   Susan will have enough money to buy a computer soon.
    ....
    ....

5   We will watch the basketball game on TV later.
    ....
    ....

Be Going To

Affirmative
I am (I'm) going to go
you are (you're) going to go
he/she/it is (he's/she's/it's) going to go
we/you/they are (we're/you're/they're) going to go

Negative
I am not (I'm not) going to go
you are not (aren't) going to go
he/she/it is not (isn't) going to go
we/you/they are not (aren't) going to go

Question
Am I going to go?
Are you going to go?
Is he/she/it going to go?
Are we/you/they going to go?

Short Answers

Yes, I am.
Yes, you are.
Yes, he/she/it is.
Yes, we/you/they are.

No, I'm not.
No, you're not.
No, he/she/it isn't.
No, we/you/they aren't.

We use *be going to*:

➤ for plans and arrangements in the near future.
He's going to buy a new car.
They are going to see their cousins in California next month.

➤ to predict something on the basis of evidence.
The brakes don't work. We're going to crash!
Look at those black clouds. It's going to rain.

Notes

We can use either *be going to* or the Future with *Will* to make predictions with little or no difference in meaning.
It's half past nine. He won't come now.
It's half past nine. He isn't going to come now.

---

3 ▷ **Make sentences with be going to and the verbs from the box.**

be   ~~fly~~   give   have   miss   rain   sell   stay   study

Ex.   I ......*am going to fly*...... *from New York to San Fancisco.*

1   They .... their house and move to a new one.
2   The bus is late so we .... the start of the movie.
3   I really don't feel well. I think I .... sick!
4   My sister .... with her friend for a few days.
5   Judging by the clouds, I think it ....
6   My boss .... us all a pay raise.
7   Our neighbors .... a barbecue this evening.
8   He .... Spanish next year.

---

4 ▷ **Complete the questions using be going to and the words in parentheses and then write answers.**

Ex.   *Are you going to make* .... *your own curtains? (you / make)* ✗
      No, I'm not. ....

1   .... that driver for speeding? (the police officer / arrest) ✓
   ....

2   .... the Pyramids in Egypt? (they / visit) ✓
   ....

3   .... the boy an injection? (the nurse / give) ✗
   ....

4   .... for a loan? (he / apply) ✓
   ....

5   .... me later this evening? (you / call) ✓
   ....

Present Continuous – Future Meaning

Affirmative
I am (I'm) leaving
you are (you're) leaving
he/she/it is (he's/she's/it's) leaving
we/you/they are (we're/you're/they're) leaving

Negative
I am not (I'm not) leaving
you are not (aren't) leaving
he/she/it is not (isn't) leaving
we/you/they are not (aren't) leaving

Question
Am I leaving?
Are you leaving?
Is he/she/it leaving?
Are we/you/they leaving?

Short Answers

Yes, I am.	No, I'm not.
Yes, you are.	No, you aren't.
Yes, he/she/it is.	No, he/she/it isn't.
Yes, we/you/they are.	No, we/you/they aren't.

We can use the Present Continuous to describe plans or arrangements in the near future.
They are leaving at six in the morning.
He isn't working next week.

Notes

We can use either *be going to* or the Present Continuous to talk about future plans and arrangements. The difference is that with the Present Continuous, we must use a phrase that shows future time unless it can be understood from the context.
They are listening to CDs. (present)
They are listening to CDs this weekend. (future)
They are going to listen to CDs. (future)

---

5 ▸ Write sentences using the Present Continuous.

Ann's list for tomorrow	
8:00	wake up
9:00	have breakfast
10:00	walk the dog
12:00	meet Jane for lunch
2:00	go shopping
5:00	make dinner
8:00	go the movies

Ex.   *Ann's waking up at 8 o'clock tomorrow.* ....

1   ....

2   ....

3   ....

4   ....

5   ....

6   ....

---

6 ▸ Write questions and answers using the verbs in parentheses.

Ex. ....*Are*........ you ....*buying*............ a birthday cake for your sister this afternoon? (buy / make)
No, I'm not. I'm making a birthday cake for my sister this afternoon.

1   .... your brother .... lunch tomorrow? (buy / make)
....

2   .... we .... to Boston this weekend? (fly / drive)
....

3   .... you .... your friend on Sunday? (call / visit)
....

4   .... you .... tennis on Friday night? (play / watch)
....

5   .... they .... to work next week? (drive / walk)
....

6   .... the dancers .... this weekend? (rehearse / perform)
....

Simple Present – Future Meaning

Affirmative
I/you work
he/she/it works
we/you/they work

Negative
I/you do not (don't) work
he/she/it does not (doesn't) work
we/you/they do not (don't) work

Question
Do I/you work?
Does he/she/it work?
Do we/you/they work?

Short Answers

Yes, I/you do.
Yes, he/she/it does.
Yes, we/you/they do.

No, I/you don't.
No, he/she/it doesn't.
No, we/you/they don't.

We can use the Simple Present to talk about schedules and programmed events in the future.
Their ferry sails at 9 p.m. this evening.
My English class is at 10 a.m. tomorrow.

---

7 ▶ **Complete the sentences with the Simple Present or the Present Continuous.**

Ex. *The ship* ......*sails*...... *at 7 o'clock tonight. (sail)*

1   Our train .... at 4 o'clock tomorrow afternoon. (depart)

2   Where .... you .... on vacation this year? (go)

3   Wendy and Michael .... a dinner party on Saturday. (have)

4   .... the bus to Dallas .... from this bus station? (leave)

5   When .... the bank .... tomorrow? (open)

6   .... he .... with us to the theater tonight? (come)

Time Expressions with Future Tenses

tomorrow	next week
the day after tomorrow	next year
soon	in a minute
later	in an hour
next Friday	in two days

Present Tenses in Time Clauses about the Future

We don't use future tenses in time clauses about the future. We use the Simple Present, the Present Continuous or the Present Perfect.

Some words that introduce future time clauses are:
when
until
while
after
before
as soon as
by the time

We use the Present Perfect when we want to emphasize that one action must finish before the next action happens.
I will call you when I have found out more information.

She won't have finished the report by the time the meeting starts.
Where will you be while they are doing the housework?
He'll be exhausted after he has done all that work.

8 Complete the sentences with the verbs from the box. Use the Future with Will, Simple Present or Present Perfect. More than one answer may be possible.

arrive	decide	do	find	have	look	visit	wait	wake

Ex. *Sarah* ....will visit............ *her grandmother when she has finished work on Friday.*

1 Will you ask her to call me when she .... up?

2 Will he go to the bank before he .... lunch?

3 As soon as I .... time, I'll walk the dog.

4 I .... until the manager is ready to see me.

5 The babysitter .... after the children while we are out on Saturday night.

6 Don't start cooking the vegetables until all the guests ....

7 By the time you .... to apply for the job, it will be taken.

8 After you .... the ironing, will you make the beds?

Comparison of Usage

future predictions (and after some phrases like *I expect, I'm sure,* etc.)	Future with *Will*
future predictions when we have proof that something will happen	*be going to*
decisions made at the time of speaking	Future with *Will*
promises, threats, invitations, offers	Future with *Will*
plans for the near future	*be going to* Present Continuous
schedules/programmed events	Simple Present

9 Choose the correct time expression.

Ex. *He'll watch the news* (before)/ *after he goes to bed.*

1 Will you have dinner ready *until / by the time* I come home tonight?

2 He hasn't called me yet. I'll let you know *as soon as / while* he does.

3 My daughter has always wanted a puppy. She won't be happy *until / after* we get one for her.

4 I won't leave the office *by the time / until* I finish the report.

5 Sorry. Mom's upstairs taking a nap at the moment. She'll call you back *by the time / as soon as* she wakes up.

6 *While / Before* the children are doing their homework, I'll cook dinner.

10 ▸ **Choose the correct answer.**

Freetown Festival – Part I

This year's Freetown Festival (Ex.) .... be great! There (1) .... something for everyone, no matter what your tastes and interests are. Theater lovers (2) .... delighted to hear that both the town's theaters (3) .... in full use during the weekend. You (4) .... be able to watch six different plays in all! The afternoon performances (5) .... at 2:30 p.m. and there will also be two evening performances – the first one at 6 p.m. and the other at 8:30 p.m. Theater director John Harvey-Lloyd promises that everything (6) .... spectacular. Tickets (7) .... be available from Thursday morning.

If you're interested in arts and crafts, you're also in for a wonderful time at the festival. This year, for the first time ever, we have organized special demonstrations by a number of experts. Hannah Bunton (8) .... free pottery lessons, Mike Dobbs (9) .... various painting techniques, and local jewelry maker, Angelica Arnold, (10) .... how she designs and makes her unique earrings and bracelets. All craft classes and demonstrations (11) .... at 4 p.m. and (12) .... for approximately one hour.

Ex.	**a** *going to*	**b** *it will*	**c** *is going to*	**d** *is*
1	**a** are being	**b** are	**c** will be	**d** are going to be
2	**a** will be	**b** are being	**c** is going to be	**d** are
3	**a** will being	**b** are	**c** are to being	**d** are going to be
4	**a** are being	**b** going to	**c** will	**d** are
5	**a** beginning	**b** begins	**c** begin	**d** are beginning
6	**a** is	**b** will be	**c** is going to	**d** be
7	**a** are going	**b** will	**c** are	**d** going to
8	**a** is giving	**b** gives	**c** be giving	**d** going to give
9	**a** will demonstrates	**b** is going demonstrate	**c** is demonstrating	**d** demonstrates
10	**a** will be explain	**b** are explaining	**c** explains	**d** will explain
11	**a** will	**b** begin	**c** are begin	**d** beginning
12	**a** finish	**b** last	**c** end	**d** start

(Ex. answer **c** *is going to* is circled)

11 ▶ Complete the text with will, be going to, the Simple Present and the Present Continuous. More than one answer may be possible.

Freetown Festival – Part II

As usual, there (Ex.) ....*will be*............ (be) competitions at the festival for flower arranging, painting, photography and embroidery. For the last three years, Mr. and Mrs. Fitzgerald have won all four of the competitions between them! (1) .... (they / win) again this year? Come along if you want to find out! Even better, why not enter yourself? If you are a lucky winner, you will win one of our fabulous prizes; you can choose from a laptop, a digital camera and video recorder, a DVD system or a complete home music system. The mayor (2) .... (judge) the entries on the second day of the festival, and from the entries we have already seen, this year's competition (3) .... (be) really exciting! The closing date for entries (4) .... (be) Wednesday, September 8th.

The final attraction at the festival is the wide variety of local and exotic food. This year chefs from several of the nearby Chinese, Italian, Indian and Thai restaurants (5) .... (create) wonderful dishes. After they (6) .... (demonstrate) their techniques, you (7) .... (be able to) sample the food for yourselves! The chefs (8) .... (bring) supplies of essential ingredients with them, so you can buy whatever you need to prepare the meal of your dreams! Cooking demonstrations (9) .... (start) at 10 p.m., 12 p.m. and 3 p.m. daily throughout the weekend. We are sure that everyone with an interest in arts and crafts (10) .... (enjoy) themselves at the festival next weekend.

Pairwork

> Work with a partner. Take turns. Ask and answer questions about the future.
> Ask each other about:
>
> ➤ what you are going to do this weekend.
> ➤ what you will do when you are retired.

Writing

Imagine you have won an all-expenses-paid trip anywhere in the world. Write a letter to a friend telling him/her about your good luck and describing what you are going to do.

Dear .... ,

You won't believe this! I've just won ....

....

....

....

....

....

....

....

....

....

I WILL HAVE EATEN THIS PIZZA BY THE TIME THE BOSS GETS BACK.

Future Continuous

Affirmative
I/you will (I'll/you'll) be looking
he/she/it will (he'll/she'll/it'll) be looking
we/you/they will (we'll/you'll/they'll) be looking

Negative
I/you will not (won't) be looking
he/she/it will not (won't) be looking
we/you/they will not (won't) be looking

Question
Will I/you be looking?
Will he/she/it be looking?
Will we/you/they be looking?

Short Answers

Yes, I/you will.
Yes, he/she/it will.
Yes, we/you/they will.

No, I/you won't.
No, he/she/it won't.
No, we/you/they won't.

We use the Future Continuous:

➤ to talk about actions in progress at a specific time in the future.
At this time tomorrow he will be traveling home by plane.
Will she be preparing the house for the guests tomorrow morning?

➤ to ask politely about someone's future plans.
Will you be playing in the golf tournament this weekend?
Will you be applying for the job?

➤ to talk about plans that will definitely happen because they are routine or programmed actions.
It's Friday today, so she'll be visiting her parents this evening.
My friend will be staying for two weeks.

---

1 ▷ Complete the sentences with the verbs from the box. Use the Future Continuous.

eat	give	meet	play	run	study	take	travel	watch

Ex. I ......*will be playing*...... golf in Spain at this time next week.

1 They .... TV at 9 o'clock this evening.

2 My best friend .... all evening because she has a test tomorrow.

3 The instructor .... them their assignments this afternoon.

4 My son .... his driving test at this time tomorrow afternoon.

5 We .... the new coach tomorrow at 9 a.m.

6 He .... his own business next year.

7 We .... around the world next year.

8 Don't call me between 7:00 and 7:30 because I .... my dinner then.

2 ▶ **Write questions and negative sentences.**

Ex. *He will be waiting for me outside the theater.*
Will he be waiting for me outside the theater?
He won't be waiting for me outside the theater.

1 They will be listening to the news at 8 o'clock.
....
....

2 The architect will be visiting the building site next week.
....
....

3 You will be driving back from Atlanta tomorrow.
....
....

4 He will be staying at his uncle's hotel next weekend.
....
....

5 The chef will be preparing dinner later today.
....
....

Future with Will or Future Continuous?

We use the Future with *Will* for predictions, offers, decisions, promises.
He'll earn a lot of money someday.
I'll make us a drink.

We use the Future Continuous for actions that will be in progress at a specific time in the future.
At this time next week, I'll be flying to Brazil.
Will you be having lunch at 2 o'clock?

3 ▶ **Choose the correct answer.**

Ex. *What .... at 7 o'clock this evening?*
   a *will you done*　　　**b** *are you do*　　　ⓒ *will you be doing*

1 .... me install this computer program?
   a Will you be help　　　**b** Will you help　　　**c** Will help

2 At 10 o'clock tomorrow morning, they .... their final exam in English.
   a will taking　　　**b** are take　　　**c** will be taking

3 I believe he .... in whatever he tries to do.
   a will be succeeding　　　**b** will succeed　　　**c** succeeding

4 The professor .... back his students' papers this afternoon.
   a will be giving　　　**b** will giving　　　**c** gives

5 I promise I .... to you every day.
   a write　　　**b** will write　　　**c** will be writing

6 Do you think it .... tomorrow?
   a will be rain　　　**b** will rain　　　**c** is raining

6

Future Perfect

Affirmative

I/you will (I'll/you'll) have left
he/she/it will (he'll/she'll/it'll) have left
we/you/they will (we'll/you'll/they'll) have left

Negative

I/you will not (won't) have left
he/she/it will not (won't) have left
we/you/they will not (won't) have left

Question

Will I/you have left?
Will he/she/it have left?
Will we/you/they have left?

Short Answers

Yes, I/you will.
Yes, he/she/it will.
Yes, we/you/they will.

No, I/you won't.
No, he/she/it won't.
No, we/you/they won't.

We use the Future Perfect when we talk about an action that will have finished before another action or before a specific time in the future.

(It's 4 o'clock now and she finishes work at 5 o'clock.)
She will have left work by 5 o'clock.

(He started reading the article half an hour ago.)
Will he have finished reading the article in an hour?

---

4 ▷ **Complete the sentences with the verbs from the box. Use the Future Perfect.**

be   clean   fall   finish   go   learn   leave   make   repair   see   wash

Ex.   She ....*will have made*........ dinner by the time I get home.

1   Everyone .... the office by 8 o'clock in the evening.

2   The technician .... my computer before I get home.

3   The movie .... by 10 o'clock.

4   The children .... their parents' cars before lunchtime.

5   In October my brother .... a teacher for two years.

6   I'm so tired that I .... to sleep before 9 o'clock.

7   By July he .... the Golden Gate Bridge in San Francisco.

8   We .... the house by the time dinner is ready.

9   In ten years that old building .... down.

10   By the time he's twenty, he .... how to drive.

5 ▷ Write questions and answers using the verbs in parentheses.

Ex. *you / paint / your bedroom / by next week? (clean up)*
Will you have painted your bedroom by next week?
No, I won't. I'll have cleaned up my bedroom by next week.

1 he / repair / his car / by the weekend (wash)
....
....

2 you / send / a lot of e-mails / by this evening (receive)
....
....

3 they / finish / their work / by Friday (start)
....
....

4 you / have / breakfast / by 8 o'clock (make)
....
....

5 we / get off / the plane / by this time tomorrow (just board)
....
....

6 she / write / a new book / by next month (read)
....
....

Future Perfect Continuous

Affirmative	Negative	Question
I will (I'll) have been doing	I will not (won't) have been doing	Will I have been doing?
you will (you'll) have been doing	you will not (won't) have been doing	Will you have been doing?
he will (he'll) have been doing	he will not (won't) have been doing	Will he have been doing?
she will (she'll) have been doing	she will not (won't) have been doing	Will she have been doing?
it will (it'll) have been doing	it will not (won't) have been doing	Will it have been doing?
we will (we'll) have been doing	we will not (won't) have been doing	Will we have been doing?
you will (you'll) have been doing	you will not (won't) have been doing	Will you have been doing?
they will (they'll) have been doing	they will not (won't) have been doing	Will they have been doing?

Short Answers

Yes, I/you will.	No, I/you won't.
Yes, he/she/it will.	No, he/she/it won't.
Yes, we/you/they will.	No, we/you/they won't.

We use the Future Perfect Continuous to talk about ongoing actions that started in the past, present or future and that will still be in progress at a certain time in the future.

By this time next year, he'll have been studying medicine for three years. (He still has several years of training to go.)
At 5 o'clock she'll have been cleaning the kitchen for two hours. (She won't be finished; the action will continue.)

6 ▶ **Complete the sentences with the Future Perfect Continuous of the verbs in parentheses.**

Ex.   *By next year they* ....*will have been learning*................... *English for eight years. (learn)*

1   Soon I .... in the same office for ten years. (work)

2   She .... in the same play for six months by the end of this week. (act)

3   By 5 o'clock we .... in the park for four hours. (sit)

4   Mrs. Jones .... in this school for fifteen years next year. (teach)

5   My brother .... the guitar for a year on his next birthday. (play)

6   By the time I finish this report, I .... for half an hour. (write)

7   The secretary .... eight hours by the time she goes home tonight. (type)

8   By this time next year, they .... in that house for twenty years. (live)

9   Don't worry. Tim .... for long by the time we arrive. (not wait)

10 In ten minutes it .... for five hours. (rain)

Time Expressions with the Future Perfect & Future Perfect Continuous

before ...	by Wednesday
by 5 o'clock	by the weekend
by next week	in a year's time
by now	in ten minutes
by the time ...	soon

---

7 ▶ **Check (✓) the correct answer.**

Ex.   *Will you have learned all this in Wednesday?* ____
      Will you have learned all this by Wednesday? __✓__

1   He will have graduated from college by the time he is twenty. ____
    He will be graduating from college by the time he is twenty. ____

2   His son will have started work in two years' time. ____
    His son will have started work for two years' time. ____

3   Will you have finished the report before the boss got here? ____
    Will you have finished the report before the boss gets here? ____

4   Will you be visiting a museum at this time next week? ____
    Will you be visiting a museum by this time next week? ____

5   What will he be doing at 6 o'clock this evening? ____
    What will he have done at 6 o'clock this evening? ____

6   She will have bought a new computer before you see her next month. ____
    She will be buying a new computer before you see her next month. ____

Future Perfect or Future Perfect Continuous?

We use the Future Perfect to talk about an action that will have finished before a specific time in the future.

In contrast, we use the Future Perfect Continuous to talk about an action that began at an earlier time and is still going on at a specific time in the future. The action is not yet complete.

By this evening she will have read the entire book.
By this evening he will have been reading the book for five weeks. It's a long book. He's only halfway through it.

8 ▷ **Choose the correct answer.**

Ex.   They .... their meeting by 6 o'clock.
  a *will be starting*   ⓑ *will have started*   **c** *will have been starting*

1   By the time you get here, we .... the whole house.
  a will have been cleaning   **b** will have cleaned   **c** will clean

2   Don't worry! We .... making the meal before the guests arrive.
  a will have been finishing   **b** will be finishing   **c** will have finished

3   She .... for three hours by 7 o'clock.
  a will have been reading   **b** will be reading   **c** will read

4   Next week they .... for ten years.
  a will have been married   **b** will have been marrying   **c** will marry

5   They .... in Japan for a year in December.
  a will have live   **b** will have been living   **c** will live

6   At 9 o'clock he .... for nine hours without a break.
  a will work   **b** will have been working   **c** will be working

7   By 2005 Jane .... at Yale University for five years.
  a will have been teaching   **b** will be taught   **c** will teach

8   Do you think the plane .... already?
  a will have been leaving   **b** will have left   **c** will leave

Comparison of Usage

to talk about actions that will be in progress at a specific time in the future	Future Continuous
to ask politely about future plans	Future Continuous
to talk about actions that will have been completed before a specific time in the future	Future Perfect
to talk about actions that started in the past, present or future and that will still be in progress at a specific time in the future	Future Perfect Continuous
to talk about plans that are definite because they are routine or programmed actions	Future Continuous

9 ▸ **Find the mistakes and rewrite the sentences correctly.**

Ex. *By 9 o'clock they will be working for six hours.*
By 9 o'clock they will have been working for six hours.

1   Tomorrow at 11 o'clock we will have been flying to Costa Rica.

....

2   Will you have do all your homework by 10 o'clock this evening?

....

3   What will he have been learning by the time he is thirty years old?

....

4   We'll all be watched the basketball finals on Saturday afternoon.

....

5   Dinner will already have being cooked by the time you arrive.

....

6   By the time the tennis match ends, they'll have be playing five long sets.

....

10 ▸ **Find the extra word in each sentence and write it on the dotted line.**

Ex. *The new school will have be finished by the end of the summer.* ......*have*......

1   I won't have written my letters before time the taxi arrives. ....

2   Will you have been doing learning English for seven years by the end of this year? ....

3   Will Jack have be using the car this evening? ....

4   How will you have be traveling when you tour Australia? ....

5   My friends will they have been living in Los Angeles for three months by the end of August. ....

6   We will to have made some new friends before the end of the summer. ....

7   What will they be being doing later this evening? ....

8   It will have be raining when the plane arrives in Beijing. ....

11 ▸ **Complete the sentences in your own words using the verb form in parentheses.**

Ex. *At this time tomorrow I* .... *will be studying math* .... *(Future Continuous)*

1   When I get to work today, my boss .... (Future Continuous)

2   In ten years' time I .... (Future Perfect)

3   By 10 p.m. tonight my friends and I .... (Future Perfect Continuous)

4   By tomorrow morning I .... (Future Perfect Continuous)

5   At 3 p.m. tomorrow I .... (Future Continuous)

6   Before the weekend I .... (Future Perfect)

7   I'm sure I .... (Future with Will)

8   By this time next week, my cousin .... (Future Perfect)

Pairwork

Work with a partner. Take turns. Ask and answer questions about the following:

➤ all the things you will have done by the end of the week.
➤ what you will have been doing by August and for how long.
  For example: *By August I will have been wearing my summer clothes for two months.*

Writing

Write an article for your favorite magazine about all the things you will have done by the time you are twenty years older than you are now.

....
....
....
....
....
....
....
....
....
....
....
....
....
....
....
....

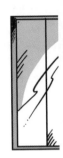

Passive Voice

The passive voice is made with the appropriate form of the auxiliary verb *to be* and the past participle of the main verb.

Verb Form	Active Voice	Passive Voice
Simple Present	*He writes the e-mails.*	*The e-mails are written.*
Present Continuous	*He is writing the e-mails.*	*The e-mails are being written.*
Simple Past	*He wrote the e-mails.*	*The e-mails were written.*
Past Continuous	*He was writing the e-mails.*	*The e-mails were being written.*
Present Perfect	*He has written the e-mails.*	*The e-mails have been written.*
Past Perfect	*He had written the e-mails.*	*The e-mails had been written.*
Future with *Will*	*He will write the e-mails.*	*The e-mails will be written.*
Future Perfect	*He will have written the e-mails.*	*The e-mails will have been written.*
be going to	*He is going to write the e-mails.*	*The e-mails are going to be written.*
Infinitive	*He needs to write the e-mails.*	*The e-mails need to be written.*
Gerund (*-ing* form)	*He likes people sending him e-mails.*	*He likes being sent e-mails.*
Modals (present)	*He must write the e-mails.*	*The e-mails must be written.*

We change a sentence from active to passive voice in the following way:

➤ The object of the active sentence becomes the subject of the passive sentence.
➤ We use the verb *to be* in the same form as the verb in the active sentence.
➤ We use the past participle of the main verb in the active sentence.
➤ We use *by* if we want to say who performed the action.

She trains the guide dogs. ➜ *The guide dogs are trained by her.*
The head chef prepares the sauces. ➜ *The sauces are prepared by the head chef.*

Notes

The verb *let* is used in active sentences, but the verb *allow* is used in passive sentences.
They let us go into the concert for free yesterday. ➜ *We were allowed to go into the concert for free yesterday.*

The verbs *hear, see* and *make* are followed by a base form in active sentences, but in passive sentences they are followed by an infinitive (*to* + base form).
She made her daughter clean her room. ➜ *Her daughter was made to clean her room.*

We use the passive voice:

➤ when we want to emphasize the action rather than the person who performed it.
The new DVD shop was opened last week.

➤ when we don't know who performed the action.
Their house was painted last week.

➤ when it's obvious who performed the action.
The car thieves have all been arrested. (by the police)

Notes

We don't use the passive voice in the Present Perfect Continuous, Past Perfect Continuous, Future Continuous or Future Perfect Continuous.

The verb *to get* can be used instead of the verb *to be* in everyday speech.
His car got damaged when he left it in the parking lot.

---

1   Complete the sentences using the passive voice in the Simple Present, the Present Continuous, the Simple Past or the Past Continuous.

Ex.   *His car* .... *is serviced* .... *by an excellent mechanic every twelve months. (service)*

1   The sales figures .... by our accountant last week. (check)

2   The director's letters .... by his secretary every day. (type)

3   Toyotas and Hondas .... in Japan. (make)

4   Our dogs .... by our neighbors while we're away. (feed)

5   The coffee we drink .... in Brazil. (grow)

6   Our air conditioner .... yesterday. (repair)

7   I'll call you later. Our grass .... by the gardener now, and I can't hear a thing you're saying! (cut)

8   Gazpacho is a soup that .... cold. (eat)

9   Her wedding dress .... by a French designer. (design)

10   I didn't go to work yesterday. My house .... so I had to stay home all day. (paint)

2   Complete the sentences using the passive voice in the Present Perfect or the Past Perfect.

Ex.   *All these books* .... *have been written* .... *by famous authors. (write)*

1   The grass .... before I got home. (cut)

2   My bike .... before the day of the big bike race. (repair)

3   The bank .... several times before yesterday's failed attempt. (rob)

4   The meal .... by the time the guests arrived. (prepare)

5   The theft .... , so the police will be here soon. (report)

6   The paintings .... in a safe place while the museum is being painted. (put)

7   I think his new book .... (already publish)

8   The baby .... by 5 o'clock. (feed)

3 ▶ Write the words in the correct order to make sentences.

Ex. *before / my / week / computer / be / next / repaired / must*
My computer must be repaired before next week.

1 being / actress / questions / asked / personal / hates / the

....

2 been / plans / their / will / made / already / have

....

3 dog / by / the / car / had / a / hit / been

....

4 finished / be / before / report / Friday / this / must

....

5 will / the / the / have / wedding reception / food / eaten / been / ends / before

....

6 given back / English / will / our / next / exam / be / week

....

7 was / last / the / week / factory / demolished / old

....

8 be / telephone / will / the / paid / tomorrow / bill

....

Passive Voice – Questions and Negatives

Negatives are formed by putting the word *not* after the first auxiliary verb.
The broken window was not (wasn't) repaired today.

Questions are formed by putting the first auxiliary verb before the subject.
Their reports will be read tomorrow. → *Will their reports be read tomorrow?*

4 ▶ Write questions.

Ex. *These vegetables should be eaten soon.*
Should these vegetables be eaten soon?

1 This work has to be finished by the end of the week.

....

2 Their car will have been repaired before they go on vacation.

....

3 His car was made in Japan.

....

4 This book was written by a Brazilian author.

....

5 The house had been sold before they saw it.

....

6 Those apartments are painted every two years.

....

5 ▷ **Write questions and answers using the prompts.**

Ex. *the cows / milk / once / a day (twice) (Simple Present)*
Are the cows milked once a day?
No, they aren't. They are milked twice a day.

1   the fruit / pick / by the children (the farmer) (Simple Present)
....
....

2   your car / repair / by Wednesday (Friday) (Future with *Will*)
....
....

3   the meeting / hold (postpone) (Present Perfect)
....
....

4   the employees / pay / now (tomorrow) (Present Continuous)
....
....

5   two people / kill / in the car crash (injure) (Simple Past)
....
....

6   the computer / repair / tomorrow (next week) (Future with *Will*)
....
....

6 ▷ **Change the following sentences from active to passive voice.**

Ex. *Peter found the missing key.*
The missing key was found by Peter.

1   Mrs. Jones will teach French and English.
....

2   The new employee has done all the filing.
....

3   A local carpenter made our new furniture.
....

4   The cat is chasing a mouse.
....

5   Ben might paint the kitchen.
....

6   By 8 o'clock the president will have given a speech.
....

7   Yesterday morning the gardener was watering the plants.
....

8   Thousands of tourists visit New York every year.
....

Thinkabout**it**

It is the verb **to be** that shows the tense in passive voice. The past participle of the main verb never changes.

7 Change the following sentences from passive to active voice.

Ex. *The posters will be painted by the children.*
   The children will paint the posters.

1 The dishes hadn't been done by Janet.

....

2 The criminal is going to be interviewed by the reporter.

....

3 The doctor was asked for his advice by the nurse.

....

4 The reports will have been prepared by the secretary before the end of the day.

....

5 The package might not be delivered by the messenger service today.

....

6 The windows need to be washed by our local window washer.

....

7 This e-mail was sent by my friend.

....

8 Our garbage is collected by sanitation workers.

....

8 Find the extra word in each sentence and write it on the dotted line.

Ex. *Will the designs have done been drawn up by Friday?* .... *done* ....

1 The surprise party was been arranged by all her friends. ....

2 Jim was made to be clean his room last week. ....

3 Our house has it been bought by a couple from California. ....

4 He will be been given a prize for his bravery. ....

5 My grandmother has been being taken to the hospital. ....

6 Will the damage to have been repaired by next week? ....

7 People without tickets won't not be allowed into the stadium. ....

8 The old oak tree was been blown down by the strong winds last night. ....

Impersonal and Personal Passive Structures

The verbs *believe, consider, know, report, say, think, understand,* etc., are used in impersonal and personal structures in the passive voice.

➤ Impersonal: *It* + passive verb + *that* + clause
They say she is a champion swimmer. ➜ *It is said that she is a champion swimmer.*
They say she was a champion swimmer. ➜ *It is said that she was a champion swimmer.*
They say she is training hard. ➜ *It is said that she is training hard.*
They say she was swimming by the time she was two. ➜ *It is said that she was swimming by the time she was two.*

➤ Personal: Personal subject (e.g., *She / John / The boys*) + passive verb + infinitive
When the sentence is about the present or the future, we use present infinitives (*to* + base form or *to be* + *-ing*).
They say she is a champion swimmer ➜ *She is said to be a champion swimmer.*
They say she is training hard. ➜ *She is said to be training hard.*

When the sentence is about the past, we use perfect infinitives (*to have* + past participle or *to have been* + *-ing*).
They say she was a champion swimmer. ➜ *She is said to have been a champion swimmer.*
They say she was swimming by the time she was two. ➜ *She is said to have been swimming by the time she was two.*

Notes

Study these examples of present and perfect infinitives:

Present (Simple) ➜ *to make*
Present (Continuous) ➜ *to be making*

Perfect (Simple) ➜ *to have made*
Perfect (Continuous) ➜ *to have been making*

---

9 ▸ **Rewrite the sentences using impersonal and personal passive structures.**

Ex. *People say that she has decided to stop acting.*
It .*is said that she has decided to stop acting.*...
She ..*is said to have decided to stop acting.*...

1 People think that the bank robber has fled the country.

It ....

The bank robber ....

2 They say that Julia Roberts is one of the richest female movie stars in the world.

It ....

Julia Roberts ....

3 They believe that Shakespeare was the greatest writer of all time.

It ....

Shakespeare ....

4 People know that Michael Schumacher is an excellent racing driver.

It ....

Michael Schumacher ....

5 They think that a reporter was interviewing him when the fire started.

It ....

A reporter ....

10 Rewrite the sentences using the words given. Use between two and five words.

Ex. *People drink fruit juice all over the world.* **drunk**
Fruit juice ....*is drunk*.................................. *all over the world.*

1 No one has watered the plants yet. **been**
The plants .... yet.

2 The guide gave the tourists a list of hotels. **given**
The tourists .... a list of hotels.

3 People say that Mike's band is playing on Saturday night. **to**
Mike's band .... on Saturday night.

4 Pablo Picasso painted that picture. **by**
That picture .... Pablo Picasso.

5 Mary doesn't like people photographing her. **photographed**
Mary doesn't like ....

6 You must put all the gym equipment away before you leave. **be**
All the gym equipment .... before you leave.

7 The police still haven't found our car. **has**
Our car .... by the police.

8 Karen is reported to be missing. **that**
It is reported ....

11 Check (✓) the correct sentence.

Ex. *The milk will have been drunk by this time tomorrow.* ✓
The milk will have being drunk by this time tomorrow. ____

1 The escaped prisoner is be pursued by the police. ____
The escaped prisoner is being pursued by the police. ____

2 My friends were proud when I was presented with the award. ____
My friends were proud when I have been presented with the award. ____

3 It is said to be one of the greatest tennis players of all time. ____
He is said to be one of the greatest tennis players of all time. ____

4 My brother hates being laughed at. ____
My brother hates is being laughed at. ____

5 Will the sofas been cleaned by the weekend? ____
Will the sofas have been cleaned by the weekend? ____

6 I would like my bedroom to be painted. ____
I would like my bedroom to being painted. ____

7 Those apartments have been sold last month. ____
Those apartments were sold last month. ____

8 The tourists were being showed around the city. ____
The tourists were being shown around the city. ____

12 ▶ **Complete the text by writing one word in each blank.**

Dear Mara,

You'll never guess what happened! Remember I told you that I (Ex.) ....*had*.......... been asked to paint some pictures for an exhibition at that new art gallery which was (1) .... last month by the Mayor? Well, I managed to sell every single painting! I took my sister along to see the exhibition last Wednesday and was surprised that my work was nowhere to (2) .... seen.

I was (3) .... the good news by the curator: the paintings had all (4) .... sold the day before and (5) .... being sent that morning to their new owner. He says the paintings (6) .... be hung in the lobby of a hotel she runs. It's exciting, isn't it? One was even (7) .... for $3,000. I can't believe that things are starting to happen for me at last. It wasn't long ago that my work was (8) .... rejected by galleries.

Well, that's all for now. E-mail me soon with your news.
Best wishes,
James

Pairwork

Work with a partner. Tell each other about:

➤ things that are done in your house and who they are done by.
   For example: *The beds are made by my wife. The cooking is done by me.*
➤ things that will be done in the area where you live before the end of the year.
   For example: *New trees will have been planted in the parks. The streets will have been cleaned.*

Writing

Imagine you are the trainer of an athlete or a football/baseball/basketball team. Write a short report about all the things that have been done, will be done, need to be done, etc., in order for the athlete or the team to be ready for the next big game or event. Use the passive voice and as many verb forms as possible.

....
....
....
....
....
....
....
....
....
....

8 Adjectives & Adverbs

NORMAN'S BOSS WAS DELIGHTED WITH THE PRESENT HE GOT.

Comparison of Adjectives

Adjective	Comparative	Superlative
short	shorter	the shortest
young	younger	the youngest
large	larger	the largest
nice	nicer	the nicest
fit	fitter	the fittest
big	bigger	the biggest
busy	busier	the busiest
pretty	prettier	the prettiest
beautiful	more beautiful	the most beautiful
intelligent	more intelligent	the most intelligent

We can use the comparative to compare two people or things.
You are taller than my cousin.
Pam's bike is faster than mine.

We can use the superlative to compare one person or thing with others in a group.
Michael is the most intelligent person in our office.
This is the tallest building in the city.

Some adjectives have irregular comparative and superlative forms.

good	➜ *better*	➜	*the best*
bad	➜ *worse*	➜	*the worst*
much	➜ *more*	➜	*the most*
many	➜ *more*	➜	*the most*
little	➜ *less*	➜	*the least*
far	➜ *farther/further*	➜	*the farthest/the furthest*

Notes

The comparative and superlative form of some two-syllable adjectives like *clever, friendly, gentle, narrow* and *stupid* can be made by adding *-er/-est* or by adding the words *more/most*.
He is gentler with the baby than his brother. = He is more gentle with the baby than his brother.
She's the friendliest person I know. = She's the most friendly person I know.

1 ▶ Complete the sentences with the comparative or the superlative form of the adjectives in parentheses.

Ex. *This sofa is* ....*more comfortable*............ *than the old one. (comfortable)*

1 I'm definitely .... than my brother. (lazy)

2 I bought .... souvenir I could afford. (expensive)

3 That garden is the .... in this area. (big)

4 I think Tom Hanks is a .... actor than Tom Cruise. (talented)

5 I can't say this is .... book I've ever read. (interesting)

6 The meal you made us last night was .... ever! (good)

7 The weather was .... than the mountaineers expected. (bad)

8 Who is .... person you have ever talked to? (old)

9 He is .... at this kind of exercise than me. (good)

10 My house is .... away from work than yours. (far)

2 ▶ Find the mistakes and rewrite the sentences correctly.

Ex. *He made us the larger pizzas we'd ever seen.*
    He made us the largest pizzas we'd ever seen.
    ....

1 It seems hottest today than it was yesterday.
    ....

2 This bag is more nice than the one I bought last week.
    ....

3 She's in good shape than me; she goes to the gym every day.
    ....

4 He told us one of the fascinating stories we'd ever heard.
    ....

5 I think grammar exercises are difficult than vocabulary exercises.
    ....

6 Acting is the more challenging than being a professional athlete.
    ....

7 The weather is most refreshing today than it was yesterday.
    ....

8 He's one of the most strongest weightlifters I've ever seen.
    ....

Comparison of Adverbs

When an adverb has the same form as the adjective, it also has the same comparative and superlative forms.

early → earlier → the earliest
fast → faster → the fastest
hard → harder → the hardest
high → higher → the highest
late → later → the latest

When an adverb ends in -*ly*, we use *more* to make the comparative and *most* to make the superlative.

beautifully → more beautifully → the most beautifully
efficiently → more efficiently → the most efficiently

Some adverbs have irregular comparative and superlative forms.

badly → worse → the worst
far → farther/further → the farthest/the furthest
little → less → the least
much → more → the most
well → better → the best

3 ▷ **Choose the correct answer.**

Ex. *At the end of the race I was breathing .... than you.*

    a heavilier   **(b)** *more heavily*   **c** *most heavily*

1   I solved the crossword puzzle in yesterday's paper .... than usual.

     a easily   **b** most easily   **c** more easily

2   My boss gives me reports to write .... than she used to.

     a more frequently   **b** frequently   **c** most frequently

3   The door on our garage opens ....

     a more automatic   **b** most automatically   **c** automatically

4   He said he was .... grateful for our help.

     a more deeply   **b** deeply   **c** deeper

5   My cousin recovered from her operation .... than anyone had expected.

     a good   **b** well   **c** better

6   He was arrested because he was behaving ....

     a suspiciously   **b** most suspicious   **c** more suspiciously

4 ▷ **Complete the sentences with the superlative form of the adverbs in parentheses.**

Ex. *Who ran the race ....the most quickly..........? (quickly)*

1   Of all the people in our family, Grandad walks .... (slowly)

2   The person who plays his music .... is my brother. (loudly)

3   Jane is the secretary who writes .... (neatly)

4   Of all the dogs in the street, our dog barks .... (fiercely)

5   The best rooms go to those who reserve .... (early)

6   I run .... of all my friends. (fast)

7   The person who drives .... is my brother. (carefully)

8   My nephew works .... in his class. (hard)

Other Types of Comparison

➤ *(not) as ... as*
We use *as ... as* when two people or things are similar in some way.
She's as tall as her brother.

We use *not as ... as* when one person or thing has less of a particular quality than another person or thing.
He isn't as brave as his cousin.

➤ *less / the least*
We use *less* + adjective/adverb + *than* when one person or thing has a particular quantity to a smaller degree than another person or thing.
This book is less interesting than the one I read last week.

We use *the least* + adjective/adverb when one person or thing has less of a particular quantity than any other people or things in a group.
This book is the least interesting of all the books I've read.

➤ *comparative + and + comparative*
We use comparative + *and* + comparative to show that something is constantly increasing or decreasing.
I got hungrier and hungrier as time went by.
The company's profits have been getting smaller and smaller.

➤ *the + comparative ..., the + comparative*
We use *the* + comparative ..., *the* + comparative to show that as one thing increases or decreases, another thing is affected in a similar or opposite way.
The more you eat, the fatter you become.
The less you spend, the more you save.

---

5 ▸ **Choose the correct answer.**

Ex. *This cake is .... tasty than the one we ate last week.*

   a *least*   (**b**) *less*   **c** *most*

1   My jacket isn't .... expensive as yours.

   a as   **b** more   **c** less

2   The more it rains, the .... we feel.

   a more unhappier   **b** less happier   **c** unhappier

3   She gave me the .... exciting present of all: a pair of socks!

   a least   **b** less   **c** more

4   Our grammar skills get better and .... every week.

   a best   **b** good   **c** better

5   People eat less .... now than they used to.

   a healthy   **b** healthily   **c** healthier

6   Now that her nephew is older, he doesn't behave .... childishly as he used to.

   a as   **b** much   **c** such

7   I'm .... as chubby as I used to be when I was a teenager.

   a less   **b** not   **c** much

8   They became .... and more tired as the game continued.

   a much   **b** most   **c** more

6 ▶ **Check (✓) the correct sentence.**

Ex. *Which are the faster animals in the world?* ____
    Which are the fastest animals in the world? _✓_

1   He was a fastest runner when he was young. ____
    He was a fast runner when he was young. ____

2   By the end of the marathon we were walking slowly. ____
    By the end of the marathon we were walking slow. ____

3   It got hotter and hottest as the weeks went by. ____
    It got hotter and hotter as the weeks went by. ____

4   George isn't as intelligent as Fred. ____
    George isn't more intelligent as Fred. ____

5   I slept less peacefully last night than the night before. ____
    I slept least peacefully last night than the night before. ____

6   David is the less careful of all the children. ____
    David is the least careful of all the children. ____

7   The children acted good in the school play. ____
    The children acted well in the school play. ____

8   The noisier the children got, the angriest the teacher became. ____
    The noisier the children got, the angrier the teacher became. ____

Compound Adjectives

Compound adjectives are two or more words that act as a single adjective. They are usually joined with a hyphen. The most common compound adjectives are made with a number and a noun in the singular.

She's twenty years old. → *She's a twenty-year-old woman.*
That saw is for two men. → *That's a two-man saw.*
This book has ninety pages. → *This is a ninety-page book.*

7 ▶ **Rewrite each sentence using a compound adjective.**

Ex. *I walked for two miles.*
    I went for a two-mile walk.

1   This book has seventy pages.

    ....

2   This baby is three months old.

    ....

3   She bought a bag of flour that weighed two pounds.

    ....

4   Janet had to write a report of five hundred words.

    ....

5   We went on a train ride that lasted for thirty-five minutes.

    ....

6   We had a meal last night that had four courses.

    ....

Thinkaboutit

When a plural noun is used in a compound adjective, it becomes singular.

Adjectives with Prepositions

Some adjectives are followed by prepositions.

absent from	fond of
afraid of	frightened of
angry with	full of
ashamed of	good at
bad at	interested in
bored with/by	jealous of
capable of	pleased with
crazy about	proud of
cruel to	related to
delighted with	responsible for
famous for	similar to
fed up with	suspicious of

8 ▷ **Complete the sentences with a preposition.**

Ex.   *My parents were very proud ....of.......... me when I graduated college.*

1   The rise in the price of fruit and vegetables is related .... the recent bad weather.

2   Why are you afraid .... dogs?

3   You ought to be ashamed .... the way you behaved!

4   The walls of her son's bedroom are full .... posters.

5   It's not nice to be jealous .... anybody.

6   Who is responsible .... cleaning out the canary's cage?

7   My friend and I are crazy .... basketball.

8   My mother was delighted .... the new scarf we bought her.

9   Why were you absent .... school yesterday?

10   Personally I'm not fond .... watching sports on TV.

11   I'm fed up .... listening to your boring stories!

12   Are you as good .... drawing as your brother is?

Adverbs of Manner

Adverbs of manner show us the way in which something is done. They answer the question *how?*

quick	➜	*quickly*	*early*	➜	*early*	*high*	➜	*high*
simple	➜	*simply*	*fast*	➜	*fast*	*late*	➜	*late*
beautiful	➜	*beautifully*	*good*	➜	*well*	*near*	➜	*near*
easy	➜	*easily*	*hard*	➜	*hard*			

(How does she sing?) *She sings beautifully.*
(How does he drive?) *He drives fast.*

Adverbs of Place

Adverbs of place answer the question *where?*
(Where is the bag?) *The bag is over there.*
(Where shall I wait for you?) *Wait for me outside.*

Adverbs of Time

Adverbs of time answer the question *when?*
(When did you arrive?) *I arrived yesterday.*
(When are you going to town?) *I'm going to town later.*

Notes

When we have two or more adverbs or adverbial prepositional phrases in a sentence, they usually come in the following order:
manner – place – time
She waited patiently in front of the bank for half an hour.

When there are verbs in the sentence that show movement (*come, go, leave*, etc.), the order is:
place – manner – time.
I drove to work carefully this morning because the roads were icy.

Adverbs of Degree

Adverbs of degree show us the strength or intensity of the adverb or adjective they modify. They answer the question *how much* or *to what extent?*

enough
quite
rather
too
so
very/really
extremely
completely
absolutely

adjective/adverb + *enough* + full infinitive
He isn't stupid enough to fight.
They didn't work hard enough to pass their exams.

quite + adjective/adverb
It's quite cold today.
He works quite hard.

rather + adjective/adverb
This recipe is rather difficult to follow.
She speaks rather fast.

too + adjective/adverb + full infinitive
She is too selfish to share her chocolate.
They walked too slowly to get to the bus stop in time.

so + adjective/adverb
Don't shout so loudly!
I didn't know you sang so well.

very/really + adjective/adverb
You're a very/really kind person.
The chef cooks very/really well.

extremely + adjective/adverb
She was extremely bored.
We tried extremely hard.

completely + verb/adjective
He completely supports me in my decisions.
I feel completely different about it today.

absolutely + adjective
He made it absolutely clear that we had to leave.

9 ▷ **Choose the correct word.**

Ex.   *It is* such / (so) *hot today that I'm going to go swimming.*

1   She cooks *too / extremely* well.
2   That book I've just read was *enough / rather* boring.
3   Most of my friends are old *enough / quite* to drive a car.
4   This program is *enough / quite* interesting.
5   I'm feeling *enough / too* lazy to go to work today.
6   The tour guide was *too / quite* glad when we said we enjoyed the museum.
7   Children can be *so / enough* unkind sometimes.
8   We went to a(n) *extremely / too* good concert last night.
9   I'm feeling *enough / rather* tired this morning.
10   The earthquake *completely / really* destroyed the building.

10 > Choose the correct adverb and rewrite each sentence with the adverb in the correct place.

Ex. *I forgot about it. (completely / enough)*

I completely forgot about it.

1 She visited her cousin who lived nearby. (frequently / outside)

....

2 We missed the bus. (nearly / hardly)

....

3 My friend is waiting for me while I finish my work (rather / outside)

....

4 He checked the report and gave it to his boss. (good / carefully)

....

5 We were exhausted after the long hike. (enough / absolutely)

....

6 I was sorry to hear your news. (deeply / sadly)

....

7 He was tired when he got home, so he went straight to bed. (extremely / much)

....

8 He answered her. (extremely / angrily)

....

Pairwork

Work with a partner. Describe the following, using as many adjectives and adverbs as possible:
➤ an exciting sports event you have seen.
➤ the best/worst concert or exhibition you have ever been to.

Writing

➤ Think of the most beautiful or amazing place you have ever visited. Write a short description of it for someone who is thinking of going there. Use adjectives and adverbs from this unit.
➤ Think of the most frightening or dangerous thing you have ever done. Write a short paragraph describing it to your friend. Use adjectives and adverbs from this unit.

Review 2 (Units 5-8)

1 ▶ Complete the sentences with will and the verbs from the box.

| be | get | know | leave | not find | remember | send | spend | travel |

Ex. Dinner ....*will be*.......... ready in about half an hour.

1 I'm sure he .... too much on a new car.

2 We haven't decided how we .... to New York yet.

3 They .... any good bargains at the new boutique. It's very expensive.

4 She .... a good job when she graduates. She's very smart.

5 Hurry up, or we .... without you!

6 I wonder if you .... me when you're famous.

7 I .... e-mails to all my friends when I move to Los Angeles.

8 How .... you .... when to leave? Your watch is broken!

2 ▶ Complete the sentences with the correct form of be going to and the words in parentheses.

Ex. When ....*are you going to see*.......... her again? (you / see)

1 Are you sure they .... to the meeting? (come)

2 He .... it when he sees what you've done. (not like)

3 We .... the children to the zoo today. (take)

4 .... your laptop to the meeting? (you / bring)

5 .... the gym with us? (they / join)

6 I don't think this idea .... (work)

7 The trip .... interesting even though it's very long. (be)

8 Why .... taking piano lessons? (he / stop)

3 ▶ Choose the correct answer.

Ex. *The bus to New Haven* will leaves / (leaves) at 10 o'clock.

1 I don't think it *will be / is* easy to learn all our lines for the play by the end of the week.

2 Next weekend we *are celebrating / will celebrating* our parents' wedding anniversary.

3 His exam is *going to begins / begins* at 9 o'clock exactly.

4 I spoke to Sue last night. *We're going to go / We'll go* shopping this afternoon.

5 They *are having / will have* a dinner party at their house tonight. Did they invite you?

6 According to the weather report, it *is being / will be* very hot for the rest of the week.

7 What *is happening / is going to happen* if you can't find the receipt?

8 *Will you open / Are you opening* the door for me, please?

4 ▷ Complete the sentences with the Future Continuous.

Ex. He ....will be eating........... his dinner if you call him now. (eat)

1 I hope it .... when we wake up in the morning. (not snow)
2 The game .... in three minutes. (start)
3 I wonder what people .... in the next century. (wear)
4 Some scientists believe that people .... on Mars by the end of this century. (live)
5 I .... any cooking when we're on vacation. (not do)
6 A taxi .... for them when they arrive at Kennedy Airport. (wait)
7 .... you .... to work as soon as you've had the operation? (return)
8 For the first year the business .... only a small profit. (make)

5 ▷ Complete the sentences with the verbs from the box. Use the Future Perfect.

> close   decide   d̶o̶   dry   fall   not finish   receive   spend   write

Ex. She ....will have done.......... all her homework by the time dinner is ready.

1 When .... you .... which job to accept?
2 The post office .... by now, so we'll have to buy the stamps tomorrow.
3 You .... my letter before the end of the week.
4 They .... all their money by the time they get home.
5 I .... reading this novel before the end of the day.
6 The doctor .... about forty prescriptions by the time he leaves the office today.
7 The temperature .... to below freezing by midnight.
8 The clothes .... in an hour or two.

6 ▷ Choose the correct answer.

Ex. It (will have been raining) / will rain *for six hours non-stop in another half an hour.*

1 Where *will you live / will you have lived* when you go to college?
2 By the time the play finishes, the last bus *will be leaving / will have left.*
3 By this evening the dentist *will have been seeing / will have seen* twenty patients.
4 I *will have known / will have been knowing* my neighbors for ten years soon.
5 By tomorrow our phone *will have been / will be being* out of order for four days.
6 I *will have finished / will have been finishing* getting ready to go out in another ten minutes.
7 *Will it have stopped / Will it have been stopping* raining before we get up?
8 They *will have been drinking / will have drunk* all the orange juice before the others come to the table.

7 ▷ Choose the correct answer.

Ex. The rainfall is been / (being) *measured by the meteorologists.*

1 People in many stores are being *watching / watched* on closed-circuit TV cameras.
2 The boarding passes *was / were* being collected by a flight attendant in an orange uniform.
3 The banquet this evening is being *hold / held* in the large dining room on the top deck.
4 The equipment will *being / be* transported in a huge truck.
5 Just before we went through passport control, an announcement about the delay was *make / made* .
6 The conference *had been / was been* attended by many important scientists.
7 The seriously injured driver *was / is* rushed to the hospital in an ambulance.
8 They are *made / making* arrangements for the delayed passengers to stay in a hotel.

8 ▶ **Rewrite the sentences using the words given. Use between two and five words.**

Ex. *Calvin Klein designed the dress she is wearing tonight.* **was**
The dress she is wearing tonight ....*was designed by*............. *Calvin Klein.*

1 The director paid for the meal. **by**

The meal .... the director.

2 John has written the sales report. **been**

The sales report .... John.

3 Suzanne will play the part of the leading lady. **be**

The part of the leading lady .... Suzanne.

4 Mary made that fantastic loaf of bread. **by**

That fantastic loaf of bread .... Mary.

5 They say the problem of pollution is getting more serious. **to**

The problem of pollution .... more serious.

6 Agatha Christie wrote *The Mousetrap*. **by**

The Mousetrap .... Agatha Christie.

7 The famous designer has created an exciting new line of sportswear. **been**

An exciting new line of sportswear .... the famous designer.

8 The new spy movie is said to be really good. **that**

It .... the new spy movie is really good.

9 ▶ **Find the mistakes and rewrite the sentences correctly.**

Ex. *My bedroom needs to been painted again.*
My bedroom needs to be painted again. ....

1 I think you ought to be gave a prize for that photograph.

....

2 When I visited my aunt's house, her burglar alarm is being installed.

....

3 Their plans will they be made by the end of the month.

....

4 Our new car will had been delivered to our house by next weekend.

....

5 That report will have done written by now.

....

6 Her wedding dress was already been altered three times.

....

7 Our kitchen is be designed by an expert.

....

8 Our car is having serviced once every six months.

....

10   **Complete the sentences with the comparative or superlative of the words in parentheses.**

Ex.   *He is one of* .... *the smartest* .... *students in the school. (smart)*

1   You must drive .... than that if you don't want to have an accident.
(careful)

2   This car is the .... thing he's ever bought. (expensive)

3   They felt even .... after hearing strange noises coming from inside the empty
house. (nervous)

4   I think it is the .... movie I've ever seen. (exciting)

5   He's just set a new world record. The marathon has never been run .... (fast)

6   Surely the weather can't get any .... ! (wet)

7   Your house is one of the .... I've ever seen. (nice)

8   My brother is .... than yours. (heavy)

11   **Complete the sentences with the words from the box.**

completely   earlier   extremely   highest   ~~late~~   outside   quietly   well   yesterday

Ex.   *Everybody arrived* .... *late* ....; *we were the only ones who got there on time.*

1   I'm feeling better today than I did ....

2   They did their work .... while the boss was at a meeting.

3   They .... forgot about their appointment.

4   He played really .... and we were all proud of him.

5   You'll have to wait for me ....

6   He came .... than we'd expected, so he helped us with the preparations.

7   Whose kite flew the ....?

8   I feel .... relaxed now that I've had a month-long vacation!

12   **Choose the correct answer.**

Ex.   *I never realized you were* (so) / *such afraid of snakes.*

1   I thought you were *too / enough* old to join the youth club.

2   Why are you *such / so* angry with your cousin?

3   They were *highly / such* delighted with their presents.

4   I'm *enough / rather* fond of the idea of going to Hawaii next year.

5   I can't believe that I had to walk *such / so* quickly to keep up with him!

6   I'm hungry *too / enough* to eat at least two pieces of cake!

7   She's *very / enough* proud of her children.

8   The necklace he bought you is *absolutely / too* beautiful.

THE BOSS SAID WE SHOULDN'T WASTE TIME TALKING IN THE CORRIDOR.

Reported Statements

Direct Speech	Reported Speech
Simple Present	Simple Past
"I work in Boston," he said.	*He said he worked in Boston.*
Present Continuous	Past Continuous
"I am working in Boston," he said.	*He said he was working in Boston.*
Simple Past	Past Perfect
"I worked in Boston," he said.	*He said he had worked in Boston.*
Past Continuous	Past Perfect Continuous
"I was working in Boston," he said.	*He said he had been working in Boston.*
Present Perfect	Past Perfect
"I have worked in Boston," he said.	*He said he had worked in Boston.*
Present Perfect Continuous	Past Perfect Continuous
"I've been working in Boston," he said.	*He said he had been working in Boston.*
will	would
"I will work in Boston," he said.	*He said he would work in Boston.*
can	could
"I can work in Boston," he said.	*He said he could work in Boston.*
must	had to
"I must work in Boston," he said.	*He said he had to work in Boston.*
may	might
"I may work in Boston," he said.	*He said he might work in Boston.*

We use reported speech to tell someone what another person said.
("I am a bank manager," he said.) *He said he was a bank manager.*

The verb forms change as in the examples in the chart on the previous page.

We change personal pronouns, possessive adjectives, possessive pronouns and object pronouns.
("I trust you," she said.) *She said she trusted him.*

Notes

We often use the reporting verbs *say* and *tell* in reported speech.
Say is not followed by an object noun or pronoun.
She said she had visited Paris.

Tell is followed by an indirect object.
She told me she had been to Paris.

We can add the word *that* after the reporting verb with no change in meaning.
He said that I was a pretty girl. = He said I was a pretty girl.
I told him that I was married. = I told him I was married.

---

1 ▶ **Rewrite the sentences in reported speech.**

Ex. *"I want a bite of your sandwich!" he said.*
    He said he wanted a bite of my sandwich.

1   "They were waiting outside the museum for hours," she said.
    ....

2   "I must buy some new curtains for the living room," she told me.
    ....

3   "A florist prepares the bouquets," she said.
    ....

4   "I've been to the theater five times," he told them.
    ....

5   "They will get into trouble if they go into that building," he said.
    ....

6   "I'm studying martial arts," he said.
    ....

2 ▶ **Rewrite the sentences in direct speech.**

Ex. *They said they had traveled to France during the summer.*
    "We traveled to France during the summer," they said.

1   He said he was looking for his glasses.
    ....

2   They told her they might be home late.
    ....

3   He said he wondered how old his boss was.
    ....

4   He said he could hear a strange noise.
    ....

5   She told me she had to go to the doctor.
    ....

6   He said he had known his best friend for years.
    ....

Thinkabout**it**

Don't forget to use quotation marks in direct speech.

Changes in Time and Place

There are other changes we must make when we use reported speech.

today	→	*that day*
tonight	→	*that night*
tomorrow	→	*the following day/the next day*
yesterday	→	*the previous day/the day before*
last year	→	*the previous year/the year before*
next week	→	*the week after/the following week*
a month ago	→	*the previous month/the month before*
now	→	*then*
at the moment	→	*at that moment*
here	→	*there*
this/these	→	*that/those*

3 ▸ **Rewrite the sentences in reported speech.**

Ex. *"I'm going to meet my old history professor tomorrow," he said.*
He said he was going to meet his old history professor the following day.

1 "We aren't going on vacation this summer," she said.
....

2 "I want to watch a movie on TV tonight," he told her.
....

3 "Mark isn't here at the moment," she said.
....

4 "We may meet you in town tomorrow," he said.
....

5 "I'll wait here until you come back," she said.
....

6 "You must finish this report now," he said.
....

7 "I worked really hard yesterday," she told us.
....

8 "He was visiting his aunt last month," she said.
....

Reported Questions

The changes we make in reported statements also apply to reported questions.

When the question begins with a question word (*who, what, where, which,* etc.), we use the same question word as in the direct question.
("Why are you wearing sunglasses?" he asked.)
He asked why I was wearing sunglasses.
("Where was the bag when you last saw it?" I asked him.)
I asked him where the bag was when he had last seen it.

When the question doesn't begin with a question word, we form the reported question in the same way but we add the word *if* or *whether*.
("Do you want to come to the game with me?" he asked.)
He asked if/whether I wanted to go to the game with him.

Some of the reporting verbs we use with reported questions are *ask, wonder* and *want to know*.

Notes

Pay careful attention to word order. When changing a question from direct to reported speech, the word order of the question changes from question form to statement form.

*"What **is** your name?"* →
*He asked what my name **was**.*

4 Rewrite the questions in reported speech.

Ex. *"Where do you live," he asked me.*
He asked me where I lived.

1 "When did you go out for an Italian meal?" he asked her.

2 "Who opened the kitchen door?" she asked.

3 "Why did you move my newspaper?" he asked me.

4 "What time will it be when you arrive at your hotel?" she asked him.

5 "What are you doing this evening?" he asked me.

5 Rewrite the reported questions in direct speech.

Ex. *I asked her if she knew how to make pancakes.*
"Do you know how to make pancakes?" I asked her.

1 I asked whether it was going to rain.

2 He asked me if I had enjoyed my trip to California.

3 My brother asked me if I could wash his car.

4 The professor asked the students if they had understood his explanation.

5 I asked him if he knew where the Museum of Modern Art was.

6 Rewrite the dialogue in reported speech.

Bob: Hello, Bill. How are you today?
Bill: I'm fine. Where are you going?
Bob: I'm going downtown. I want to buy a new CD, and I may buy something for my sister.
Bill: Can I go with you? I've been wanting to go shopping for ages, so this will be a good opportunity.
Bob: Of course you can.

Ex. *Bob said hello to Bill and asked him how he was that day.*

1

2

3

4

Reported Commands & Requests

Reported commands are usually introduced with the verb *tell*
+ object + infinitive.
("Stop talking!" said the teacher to her students.)
The teacher told her students to stop talking.

If the command is negative, we put *not* in front of *to*.
("Don't shout at me!" he said.)
He told me not to shout at him.

Reported requests are usually introduced with the verb *ask*
+ object + infinitive.
("Please wait patiently," he said.)
He asked the passengers to wait patiently.

If the request is negative, we put *not* in front of *to*.
("Please don't touch the wet paint," she said.)
She asked us not to touch the wet paint.

Notes

In reported speech we omit the word *please*.
("Please help me carry my shopping," she asked.)
She asked me to help her carry her shopping.

7 ▶ **Rewrite the commands and requests in reported speech.**

Ex. *"Leave the building!" he said to the employees.*
  He told the employees to leave the building.

1 "Don't cross the road there!" she said to him.
  ....

2 "John, close the windows immediately!" she said.
  ....

3 "Please take the garbage out," said my cousin to me.
  ....

4 "Eat your spinach!" she said to her son.
  ....

5 "Please give me another chance," he said to me.
  ....

8 ▶ **Rewrite the reported commands and requests in direct speech.**

Ex. *He told her to leave the room.*
  "Leave the room," he told her.

1 She told them not to talk during the exam.
  ....

2 He told me not to get so angry.
  ....

3 He asked her not to tell anyone.
  ....

4 He told her to bring him a glass of water.
  ....

5 She asked him to buy some milk on his way home.
  ....

Other Common Reporting Verbs

Verb + infinitive

agree	"Yes, I'll help you," he said.	He agreed to help me.
offer	"Shall I help you?" he asked.	He offered to help me.
promise	"I promise I'll help you," he said.	He promised to help me.
refuse	"No, I won't help you," he said.	He refused to help me.
threaten	"Stop shouting or I'll leave," he said.	He threatened to leave if I didn't stop shouting.

Verb + object + infinitive

advise	"You should work harder," he said.	He advised me to work harder.
ask	"Could you help me?" he asked.	He asked me to help him.
beg	"Please, please help me," he said.	He begged me to help him.
command	"Stand at attention," he said.	He commanded them to stand at attention.
invite	"Will you join me?" he asked.	He invited me to join him.
order	"Leave immediately," he said.	He ordered them to leave immediately.
remind	"Don't forget to take your hat," he said.	He reminded me to take my hat.
warn	"Don't touch the fire," he said.	He warned me not to touch the fire.

Verb (+ preposition) + gerund

admit (to)	"Yes, I stole the money," he said.	He admitted (to) stealing the money.
accuse (sb) of	"You stole my wallet," he said.	He accused me of stealing his wallet.
apologize for	"I'm sorry I lied," he said.	He apologized for lying.
boast about	"I'm stronger than you," he said.	He boasted about being stronger than me.
complain (to sb) about	"I feel fed up," he said.	He complained about feeling fed up.
deny	"I didn't steal your bag," he said.	He denied stealing my bag.
insist on	"You must study tonight," he said.	He insisted on me/my studying that night.
suggest	"Let's go to the mall," he said.	He suggested going to the mall.

Verb + that

complain	"They are always late," he said.	He complained that they were always late.
deny	"I didn't lie," he said.	He denied that he had lied.
explain	"It's difficult to understand," he said.	He explained that it was difficult to understand.
exclaim/remark	"What a lovely sofa!" he said.	He exclaimed/remarked that it was a lovely sofa.
insist	"You must apologize at once!" he said.	He insisted that I apologize at once.
promise	"I promise I'll marry you," he said.	He promised that he would marry her.
suggest	"You ought to lose weight," he said.	He suggested that she (should) lose weight.

Notes

We can use *suggest* + gerund when the speaker is participating in the action.
("Let's go to a concert this evening," Harry said.)
Harry suggested going to a concert that evening.

9 ▶ Complete the sentences with the verbs from the box.

~~apologized~~   complained   denied   insisted   invited   refused   remarked

Ex. *"I'm so sorry I hurt your feelings," he said to me.*
     He ....apologized....... to me for hurting my feelings.

1 "You must pay the bill by Thursday," he told me.
   He .... that I pay the bill by
   Thursday.

2 "What a fantastic jacket!" he said.
   He .... that it was a fantastic jacket.

3 "I'm really bored," she said.
   She .... about being bored.

4 "Will you come to the movie premiere with me?" he asked me.
   He .... me to go to the movie premiere
   with him.

5 "I certainly did not steal your purse!" he said.
   He .... stealing her purse.

6 "No, I'm not going to help my sister," she said.
   She .... to help her sister.

10 ▶ Rewrite the sentences in reported speech using the verbs in parentheses.

Ex. *"Yes, I took your book," he said. (admit)*
     He admitted (to) taking my book. ....

1 "Don't ride your bike on busy streets," she said. (warn)
   ....

2 "I promise I'll help you wash the windows later," she said. (promise)
   ....

3 "You ought to exercise more," she said. (suggest)
   ....

4 "Stop making noise or I'll send you to your room," his father said. (threaten)
   ....

5 "You scratched my bike!" he said to her. (accuse)
   ....

6 "I'll stay and help you clean up," she said. (offer)
   ....

Verb Forms That Don't Change

There are some situations in reported speech when the verb forms don't change.

The Past Perfect and the Past Perfect Continuous don't change.
("They had been good friends for years," he said.)
He said they had been good friends for years.
("I had been talking on the phone for hours," she said.)
She said she had been talking on the phone for hours.

The words *would, could, might, should, ought to, used to, had better* and *must not* don't change in reported speech. The word *must* doesn't change in reported speech when it expresses deduction.
("Nina could arrive later today," she said.)
She said Nina could arrive later that day.
("He must be the best driver in the race," she said.)
She said he must be the best driver in the race.

The Simple Present doesn't have to change when the information reported is still true.
("I live in Toronto." he said.)
He said he lives in Toronto.

In the second and third conditional, the verb forms don't change. However, in the first conditional, the present tense changes to a past tense and *will* changes to *would*.
("What would you do if you lost your purse?" I asked her.)
I asked her what she would do if she lost her purse.
("If you hadn't helped me, I wouldn't have survived," he said.)
He said that if I hadn't helped him, he wouldn't have survived.
("Where will you live if you move to the USA?" I asked him.)
I asked him where he would live if he moved to the USA.

11 ▶ **Rewrite the sentences in reported speech.**

Ex. *"We had been walking for hours,"* they explained.
They explained that they had been walking for hours.
....

1 "I live in New York," she said.

....

2 "We ought to go and see her," she told me.

....

3 "We could stay home tonight," he said.

....

4 "If you saw the movie, you would like it," they said.

....

5 "If John had left earlier, he wouldn't have arrived late," Mary explained.

....

6 "Paris is the capital of France," he told the children.

....

7 "I used to be a police officer," he told his new neighbor.

....

8 "Water turns to ice at 0° Celsius," the teacher told the class.

....

Pairwork

Tell your partner four things about your family. Try to use different verb forms.
When you have finished, your partner will put them in reported speech.

For example:
My brother went to the movies last night.
He said his brother had gone to the movies the previous night.

Writing

Imagine you are a reporter for a magazine. You have recently interviewed a famous person from your country.
Write a report about the interview for the magazine. Use both direct and reported speech.

....

....

....

....

....

....

....

....

....

....

Ability – Can / Could / Be Able To

He can ride a horse.	She could swim by her fifth birthday.	They will be able to leave early.
He can't ride a motorbike.	She couldn't go to Anna's wedding.	They weren't able to find a room.
Can he ride an elephant?	Could she speak French last year?	Have they been able to ski yet?

We use *can* to talk about ability in the present.
He can fly a helicopter.
She can't drive a tractor.

We use *could* to talk about past ability.
He could speak French when he was three.
They could draw very well when they were young.

We use *be able to* to talk about ability. It can be used with all verb forms except continuous forms.
She has been able to paint portraits for years.
I hadn't been able to find the address he wanted until yesterday, when I found it by chance.

Notes

The verb *can* cannot be used with future forms like *be going to* or *will*. We must use *will be able to* to talk about ability in the future. However, when we are making decisions that refer to future ability/possibility, the word *can* may be used.
He can't see you this evening, but he can call tomorrow.

We can use *couldn't* to talk about specific or general situations. We can use both *could* or *was/had been able* to for general past ability. For a specific situation in which we managed to do something, we can only use a past form of *be able to*.
I couldn't fix the sink yesterday, but luckily the plumber was able to.

When we use verbs of sense (e.g., *see, feel, hear*), we usually use *could*, not *be able to*.
She could see her brother outside the window.

1 **Choose the correct answer.**

Ex. *I can /* could *play the piano before I started school.*

1 He *will be able to / could* walk to work when they move to Boston.

2 He *is able / can* to swim extremely fast.

3 *Were / Could* you able to speak English before you began taking lessons?

4 The printer wasn't working yesterday but luckily my colleague *could / was able to* repair it last night.

5 What *were you able / could you* do when you were three years old?

6 He said he *had been able to / had could* take notes in shorthand at the conference.

7 *Can / Are* you translate this report into French?

8 It was a clear day, so we *are able to / could* see for miles.

2 **Complete with the correct form of can, could or be able to. More than one answer may be possible.**

Ex. Who ....*is able to/can*............ help me with this article about the environment?

1 Ten years ago I .... speak English at all.

2 I .... film the wedding because I had my video camera with me.

3 .... you help me do this crossword puzzle?

4 Who .... snowboard when they were sixteen?

5 Next year I .... spend more time studying English.

6 I .... usually ski better than this!

Obligation, Necessity and Prohibition – Must / Have To

I must leave now or I'll be late. She must not leave the keys in the front door.	You have to make an appointment to see the doctor. We don't have to book a table in that restaurant. Does she have to wait for him?

We use *must* and *have to* to express obligation or necessity. We use *have to* in most verb forms, but not in the continuous forms.
You must ask for permission before you go in there.
I must make an appointment with my dentist.
He has to finish his report tomorrow.
They had to repaint the house.

We use *must not* to talk about something that is forbidden. (The form *mustn't* is rare in American English.)
You must not make a lot of noise when the baby is sleeping.

We use *don't have to* to talk about something that is not a necessity.
She doesn't have to walk to school.

Must is rarely used in questions in American English. Instead, we use the question form of *have to*.
Does she have to make her own food?
Do I have to go out tomorrow?

Notes

Must usually expresses internal obligation, whereas *have to* expresses external obligation.
I must buy some new shoes because I want to look my best at the job interview.
I have to wear a seatbelt. (If I don't, I'll pay a fine.)

We can also use *can't* for things that are forbidden. Usually *must not* is more emphatic than *can't*.
You must not eat poisonous mushrooms. (It's dangerous.)
He can't watch TV until he's had his dinner. (His parents won't let him.)

3 ▸ Write questions. (Remember: In American English we usually use **have to** in questions about obligation.)

Ex.   *I have to start making dinner now.*
      Do I have to start making dinner now? ....

1   They must make their beds every day.
    ....

2   He has to buy milk on the way home.
    ....

3   Police officers have to wear a uniform.
    ....

4   We must wash our hands before dinner.
    ....

5   I have to make lunch for everyone tomorrow.
    ....

6   She has to look after her little sister tonight.
    ....

7   He must paint his house this summer.
    ....

8   You have to wear a helmet when you're riding your motorbike.
    ....

Thinkabout**it**

We use **do/does** to
make questions
with **have/has to**.

4 ▸ Complete with **must not** or **can't**. Sometimes both are correct.

Ex.   *My boss says I ....can't........ go home early because I have to finish the report.*

1   You .... talk in the library.
2   We .... take our camera into that museum because the sign says "No cameras allowed."
3   I .... go out tonight because I don't feel well.
4   Why .... you come to the basketball game with us this evening?
5   My father used to tell me I .... waste so much time doing nothing.
6   I'd like to go with you, but I .... because I don't have enough money.
7   We .... waste our natural resources.
8   The children .... bring food into the classroom.

Permission – Can / Could / May

He can stay up late tonight. He can't have a new bike. Can we go to the movies?	Could I use your phone?	You may go to the park. You may not leave your luggage here. May I leave early today?

We use *can, could* and *may* to ask if something is allowed or not.
Can I park my car here?
Could I take a photo of this painting?
May I have tomorrow off?

We use *can* and *may* to talk about things that are allowed or are not allowed. *May* is the polite form.
You can go to the park this afternoon.
He can't leave his motorbike there.
You may borrow my car.
She may not stay here for the weekend.

Notes

We use *could* to ask for permission, but not to talk about things that are allowed or not allowed.

Requests – Can / Will / Could / Would

Can you help me for a minute, please?
Will you let me know as soon as possible, please?

Could you hold the door open, please?
Would you take these books back for me, please?

We use *can* and *will* to ask someone for something.
Can I have a glass of milk, please?
Will you lend me your bike, please?

We use *could* and *would* to ask more politely.
Could you lend me your car, please?
Would you move out of the way, please?

Notes

When we answer a question with *could* or *would*, we usually use *can* or *will*.
Could you repair my bike, please? Yes, I can. / No, I can't.
Would you pay for my lunch, please? Yes, I will. / No, I won't.

5 ► **Choose the correct answer.**

Ex. (Could) / Will *I borrow your car, please?*

1   *May / Will* I leave the room?
2   "You *could / may* leave work early this afternoon," said Jane's boss.
3   *May / Can* you hold the door open for me while I carry the new TV in, please?
4   *Will / May* you let me borrow your pen?
5   *Would / May* you take a message, please?
6   The manager said we *could / will be* go to lunch early.
7   *May / Would* I help you, sir?
8   *Can / Would* I ask you a question about your family?

Obligation and Necessity – Need To

Affirmative
I/you need to listen
he/she/it needs to listen
we/you/they need to listen

Negative
I/you don't need to listen
he/she/it doesn't need to listen
we/you/they don't need to listen

Question
Do I/you need to listen?
Does he/she/it need to listen?
Do we/you/they need to listen?

Short Answers

Yes, I/you do.	No, I/you don't.
Yes, he/she/it does.	No, he/she/it doesn't.
Yes, we/you/they do.	Yes, we/you/they don't.

We use *need to* to talk about something that is or isn't necessary to do, or to ask if something is necessary. We use it in most verb forms, but not in continuous forms.
She needs to buy a ticket before she gets on the train.
I needed to finish the report before the morning.
Have you ever needed to write a report by hand?

Notes

Need to is similar in meaning to *have to*.
I need to finish my project. = I have to finish my project.
Did he need to go home? = Did he have to go home?
We won't need to get a visa. = We don't have to get a visa.

6 ► **Complete the sentences with need to and the words in parentheses.**

Ex.   *He* ....*needed to take*............ *an aspirin because he had a headache. (take)*

1   We stopped at the bank because I .... some money. (get)
2   .... you .... this newspaper article on the environment? (keep)
3   Jane .... us with the dishes. We can manage. (not help)
4   James .... yesterday, so he stayed at home. (not go out)
5   .... you .... an umbrella when it rained yesterday? (borrow)
6   I .... a new camera. My old one is broken and can't be repaired. (buy)

7 ▶ **Choose the correct answer.**

Ex. You **must** / need *go and see the doctor about that.*

1   Do you *must* / *have to* wear a uniform at work?

2   They *must* / *had to* pay two months' rent in advance when they moved into their new apartment.

3   Do I *have* / *need to* tie my hair back when I'm working in the hotel kitchen?

4   You *have* / *must* to register for this class. You can't just turn up on the first night.

5   You *must* / *have to* not talk in the library.

6   We *must* / *need to* look after Aunt Mary until she recovers from her operation.

7   I'll *must* / *need to* buy a new suit for the wedding.

8   He *needs* / *has to* make all the decisions this week because his business partner is in the hospital.

Obligation and Necessity – Need ...? / Needn't / Needn't Have

Need I reply to her letter? Need she call him back?	He needn't go to the post office. We needn't buy eggs today.	She needn't have bought a present. They needn't have come early.

Need is also used like a modal verb, i.e., *need* + base form of verb (without *to*). In American English it is not as common as *need to*, but you will still come across it. We tend to use it in more formal situations.

We use *Need ...?* to ask if it is necessary to do something. When we answer, we often use *must* or *have to/don't have to*.
Need we pay a deposit before we rent the bike?
Yes, you must. / No, you don't have to.

We use *needn't* to say that it isn't necessary to do something.
We needn't apply for a visa. It's not required for Mexico.

We use *needn't have* + the past participle of a main verb when we did something in the past that we now realize wasn't necessary.
(You thought your boss wanted the report today so you finished it late last night. You find out today that he doesn't need it until next week.)
I needn't have stayed up past midnight to finish the report.
(You bought a laptop and then saw it online for half the price.)
I needn't have paid so much. Next time I'll check more carefully.

8 ▶ **Rewrite the sentences using the words given. Use between two and five words.**

Ex. *I was able to leave the office on time.* **need**
     I ....*didn't need to stay*....... *late at the office.*

1   It isn't necessary for you to dress up to come to dinner. **needn't**
    You .... to come to dinner.

2   Need I wear a new shirt? **to**
    .... a new shirt?

3   Kate went to pick up Pam at the airport but Tim was already there. **gone**
    Kate .... to pick up Pam at the airport because Tim was already there.

4   You don't have to come if you don't want to. **need**
    You .... if you don't want to.

5   I booked a room at the hotel but there were hardly any guests there. **have**
    I .... a room at the hotel because there were hardly any guests there.

6   I won't take my umbrella because the weather forecast is very good. **don't**
    I .... my umbrella because the weather forecast is very good.

7   It wasn't necessary for you to do so much work on this report. **done**
    You .... so much work on this report.

8   Mike is going to buy me some milk. **need**
    I .... milk as Mike is going to buy me some.

9 ▷ **Match.**

Ex. *It isn't necessary for Anne to do that now.*
1 Anne isn't able to help you now.
2 Anne needn't have done that.
3 Anne must not eat seafood.
4 Anne can't cook seafood.
5 Anne has to cook seafood.
6 Anne has prepared too much seafood.
7 It is possible for Anne to help me.
8 It isn't necessary for Anne to help me.

a She can't help you now.
b She can help me.
c She isn't allowed to eat seafood.
d She doesn't have to help me.
e She didn't need to do that.
f She didn't need to prepare so much seafood.
g She doesn't know how to cook seafood.
h She is obliged to cook seafood.
i *She doesn't need to do that now.*

10 ▷ **Find the extra word in each sentence and write it on the dotted line.**

Ex. *Can you to understand Chinese?* ......*to*......

1 I didn't need not to wait so long. ....
2 Are you be able to climb to the top of that mountain? ....
3 We don't have to going go shopping today because I went yesterday. ....
4 Could you will tell me where the new shopping center is, please? ....
5 You must not to go out in this rain without a jacket on! ....
6 I really have to need make an appointment with the doctor tomorrow. ....
7 Do we must need to write down every word the manager says? ....
8 They needn't not have been so rude to her. ....

11 ▷ **Complete the sentences in your own words.**

Ex. *At home I must* ...*lock the doors and windows at night.*.......

1 Last week I needn't have ....
2 When he was five, my brother was able to ....
3 In the evenings I have to ....
4 My parents used to say I couldn't ....
5 When I'm at work, I must not ....
6 Every afternoon I need to ....
7 In my house we don't have to ....
8 I must ....

Pairwork

Work with a partner. Take turns and tell each other about the following:
➤ four things you must do at home
➤ four things you did last month but you needn't have done
➤ four things you need permission to do
➤ four things you need to do in the next six months

Writing

Imagine you own a hotel and you are writing an information leaflet for your guests. Write a paragraph about the rules of the hotel: things your guests must and must not do; things they need to do or bring with them; and things they do not have to do or bring with them because of services the hotel will provide.

....
....
....
....
....
....
....
....
....

11 Conditionals

IF HE DOESN'T LOSE HIS JOB THIS TIME, IT WILL BE A MIRACLE.

Zero Conditional

The zero conditional is formed as follows:

If + Simple Present, + Simple Present
If you scream at the cat, it runs away.

We use the zero conditional to describe things that always happen. Sometimes we can replace *if* with *when*.
If the temperature drops to below 0° C, the lake freezes.
Snow melts when the temperature rises.

Notes

When the *if* clause comes before the result clause, it is followed by a comma. When the result clause comes before the *if* clause, no comma is needed.
If you break the law, the police arrest you.
The police arrest you if you break the law.

---

1 ▷ **Complete the sentences with the zero conditional.**

Ex. *If I ....take......... an aspirin, my headache ....goes......... away. (take, go)*

1   When people .... forests, animals .... (destroy, suffer)

2   If my sister .... too much chocolate, she .... sick. (eat, feel)

3   If he .... more than a few blocks, his knees .... (walk, hurt)

4   She .... happy when the sun .... (feel, shine)

5   If I .... late, I .... tired the next day. (stay up, feel)

6   If I .... a sad song, I .... (hear, cry)

7   When he .... careful, he .... really good reports. (be, write)

8   If the temperature .... below freezing, puddles .... to ice. (drop, turn)

First Conditional

The first conditional is formed as follows:

If + Simple Present/Present Continuous, + Future with *Will*/imperative
If you pay me, I'll wash your car.
If you're having trouble, let me know.

We use the first conditional to talk about things that will probably happen now or in the future.
If you get caught stealing, you will go to prison.
He will feel sick if he eats any more pizza.
If she gets the job, she will be really happy.

2 ▶ **Complete the sentences with the first conditional.**

Ex. *If it ....rains............. , we ....won't go.......... on a picnic. (rain / not go)*

1   My cousin .... really pleased if he .... his driving test this time. (be, pass)

2   If he .... with the police, they .... him. (not cooperate, arrest)

3   I .... you a hot drink if you .... me to. (make, want)

4   If she .... her hair cut, she .... a lot younger. (have, look)

5   He .... the final if he .... for it. (not pass / not study)

Second Conditional

The second conditional is formed as follows:

If + Simple Past/Past Continuous, + *would/could/might* + base form of main verb
If he wanted a job, he would try harder to get one.
If you were coming with us, we might have more fun.

We use the second conditional:

➤ to talk about something that is impossible.
   If I were the boss, I would give everyone a huge raise!

➤ to talk about something that is possible, but unlikely.
   If I had enough money, I would buy you a meal.

➤ to give advice, usually with the phrase *If I were you, ...*
   If I were you, I'd eat more fresh fruit.

Notes

When we use the verb *be* in the *if* clause of a second conditional sentence, we usually use *were* for all subjects.
If she were a famous actor, she would live in Los Angeles.
I'd be happier if I were lying on a beach right now!

3 ▶ **Write sentences with the second conditional.**

Ex. *he / buy / a new car / he / have / lots of fun*
     If he bought a new car, he would have lots of fun. ....

1   this job / be / more interesting / I / enjoy / it more

    ....

2   I / be / you / I / do / something / to get in shape.

    ....

3   she / speak / more languages / she / get / a better job

    ....

4   they / spend / less money / they / be able to / buy / new car

    ....

4 ▷ **Write questions with the first or second conditional.**

Ex. If there's a job open, ..._will you apply_......... for it? (you / apply)

1 If he tried harder, ... better? (he / do)

2 .... weight if he went to the gym more often? (he / lose)

3 .... with you if you ask her? (she / come)

4 If the boss doesn't explain this to us, how .... what to do?
(we / know)

5 If there are any tickets left for the concert, ... me one?
(you / buy)

6 .... the prize if he finished first? (he / get)

7 .... with the baby this evening if we can get tickets for the theater? (you / stay)

8 If I helped you, ... me your car tomorrow? (you / lend)

> **Thinkaboutit**
>
> When we make a question, the question form appears in the main clause, not in the *if* clause.

Third Conditional

If + Past Perfect/Past Perfect Continuous, + *would/could/might* + *have* + past participle
If I had heard you calling, I would have tried to help you.
If they had eaten less, they might not have felt so sick afterwards.
If he had been listening as carefully as me, he would have understood what happened.

We use the third conditional to talk about things that didn't happen, but that might have happened if the past had been different.
If he had known I was in the country, he would have called me. (He didn't know, so he didn't call.)
If he hadn't driven so fast, he might not have had the accident. (He did drive fast, and he had the accident.)

5 ▷ **Complete the sentences with the third conditional.**

Ex. If they ...._hadn't wasted_......... so much time watching TV, they .....*would have gotten/got*... better grades.
(not waste, get)

1 If I .... he was going to be here, I .... (know, not come)

2 If the new player .... so rude to everyone, he .... some
friends. (not be, make)

3 If it ...., we .... for a walk. (not rain, go)

4 My friend .... upset if I .... at him. (not be, not yell)

5 The burglar .... if the police .... so quickly.
(get away, not arrive)

6 If he .... so fast, he .... that accident. (not drive, not have)

7 I .... longer if the weather .... better. (stay, be)

8 If I .... home before you, I .... the program. (get, record)

6 ▶ Rewrite the sentences using the correct conditional.

Ex. *They didn't see the car coming, so they ran across the street.*
If they ....*had seen*........ *the car coming, they* ....*wouldn't have run*............ *across the street.*

1 Andrew doesn't work very hard, so his boss isn't very pleased with him.
If Andrew .... harder, his boss .... more pleased with him.

2 I'll probably go to Paris. Maybe I'll see the Eiffel Tower.
If I .... to Paris, I .... the Eiffel Tower.

3 He trained to become a doctor but he didn't know how hard it would be.
If he .... how hard it would be, he .... to become a doctor.

4 She always bakes a cake when people come for dinner.
If people .... for dinner, she .... a cake.

5 It's not difficult for me to write better reports; I just need to try harder.
If I .... harder, I .... better reports.

6 You ate that whole pizza. That's why you felt sick.
If you .... that whole pizza, you .... sick.

7 We have insurance, so we won't have to pay for the damage to our car.
If we .... insurance, we .... pay for the damage to our car.

8 Heating water to 100°C makes it boil.
If you .... water to 100°C, it ....

Unless, Provided/Providing (That), As Long As

We can use *unless, provided/providing (that)* and *as long as* in the first conditional.
If you don't exercise, you won't get fit.
Unless you exercise, you won't get fit.
Provided/Providing (that) you exercise, you'll get fit.
As long as you exercise, you'll get fit.

7 ▶ Rewrite the sentences using the words in parentheses.

Ex. *If I sleep well at night, I feel great the next day. (provided)*
Provided I sleep well at night, I feel great the next day.

1 Unless you apologize immediately, I'll never speak to you again! (if)
....

2 If you enjoy Chinese food, you will like the new restaurant. (as long as)
....

3 As long as we aren't late, we won't miss our flight. (unless)
....

4 Provided the weather is good, we'll have a barbecue this weekend. (if)
....

5 If you promise to be careful, I will lend you my camera. (providing)
....

6 If you don't take your medicine, you won't get better. (unless)
....

> **8** Choose the correct answer.

It's not possible to be really fit (Ex.) .... you eat properly. Just imagine! (1) .... you ate cakes and chocolate every day and you didn't eat fruit and vegetables, you (2) .... be really overweight and unfit! However, (3) .... that you eat several portions of fruit and vegetables on a daily basis, you will soon find you are fitter and healthier than you were. My boss was a perfect example of a person who doesn't eat healthily. For years he ate fast food and he didn't do any exercise. If he (4) .... eaten fresh foods more often, he would have (5) .... much healthier. But when he developed a health problem, he changed his ways. He says that (6) .... he hadn't had that problem, he wouldn't have started thinking about how important it is to eat properly. The other day I even heard him telling one of the office staff, "If you hadn't (7) .... so much junk food when you were younger, you (8) .... have had so many health problems." Luckily, my colleague wasn't offended because he's very easy-going. (9) .... he hadn't been so easy-going, he would probably (10) .... said something very rude to my boss!

Ex.	**a** *provided*	**b** *as long as*	**c** *unless*
1	**a** Unless	**b** If	**c** When
2	**a** would	**b** are	**c** do
3	**a** providing	**b** if	**c** as long as
4	**a** has	**b** would	**c** had
5	**a** be	**b** been	**c** was
6	**a** when	**b** unless	**c** if
7	**a** eat	**b** ate	**c** eaten
8	**a** would	**b** wouldn't	**c** hadn't
9	**a** Unless	**b** If	**c** When
10	**a** have	**b** had	**c** would

> **9** Find the extra word in each sentence and write it on the dotted line.

Ex. *If I go out tonight, I will be wear my new jeans and a T-shirt.* ....*be*.......

1 What would you have been done if I had told you I was leaving? ....

2 They would have be better if they rehearsed more. ....

3 If he didn't train so regularly, he wouldn't be being such a fast swimmer. ....

4 I wouldn't have worried so much if you had called unless to let me know where you were. ....

5 I'll get into a good college providing if that I get good enough grades. ....

6 How do you feel when it is snows? ....

7 Will you come to the theater with me if I would pay for the tickets? ....

8 Where would you live if you did had more money? ....

9 You won't be able to use the computer unless I not tell you my password. ....

10 She would have bought two of those bags if she'd had known how useful they would be. ....

10 ▶ **Complete the sentences in your own words.**

Ex. *If I lived in the USA,* *I would visit Disneyland regularly.* ....

1 If my boss gave me a big bonus, ...

2 Provided I eat more healthily, ...

3 If my house were too small, ...

4 If I feel anxious, ...

5 I would have worked harder if ....

6 If I learn how to fly a plane, ...

7 I will buy myself something nice providing ....

8 My family would have been amazed if ....

Pairwork

Work with a partner. Take turns. Ask and answer questions with zero, first, second and third conditionals. For example: *If you feel frightened at night, what do you do? If you won a thousand dollars, what would you do?*

Writing

Write a short composition about what you would do if your boss told you that you had to go to the USA immediately to start a new job with a high salary. Write about how you would feel, what you would have done to be prepared if you had known you were going to work in the USA, and what you would do if you had problems with the language, etc. Try to use as many types of conditional sentences as you can.

I'M GOING HOME NOW, NORMAN. HERE'S A SANDWICH IN CASE YOU GET HUNGRY LATER.

Relative Clauses

Relative clauses give us more information about the person, animal or thing mentioned in the main clause. Relative clauses begin with a relative pronoun like *who, that, which, whom* and *whose* or a relative adverb like *where* and *when*.

We use:

➤ *who/that* to talk about people.
I've met a man who/that is very interesting.

➤ *that/which* to talk about animals and things.
This is the DVD that/which we watched yesterday.

➤ *whose* to say that something belongs to somebody or something.
Is she the woman whose house was damaged in the flood?
Is that the hospital whose doctors were on strike last week?

➤ *where* to talk about places. It can be replaced with *at/in/on which*.
That's the hospital where I had my operation.
That's the hospital in which I had my operation.

➤ *when* to talk about time.
2002 was the year when I first visited the USA.

Notes

We can use *whom* when the relative pronoun is the object of the sentence when we are talking about people. We rarely use *whom* in everyday speech.
The police officer I reported the theft to was very helpful.
The police officer whom I reported the theft to was very helpful.

When there is a preposition before the relative pronoun, we must use *whom* and not *who*.
The police officer to whom I reported the theft was very helpful.

Sometimes the relative pronoun can be omitted. For more information, see *Defining Relative Clauses: Notes* on page 91.

1 ▶ Choose the correct answer.

Ex. *Mom is paying the man* what / (who) *repaired our dishwasher.*

1 Fall is the season *which / when* leaves change color and fall from the trees.

2 What did the person to *who / whom* you gave the money look like?

3 Are those the books *what / that* you got from the second-hand bookstore?

4 The reason *for / why* he can't play in the game is that he injured his ankle.

5 Is this the building *which / where* they store their furniture in?

6 Is that the factory *which / where* they make cars?

7 2005 was the year in *which / when* he graduated college.

8 Do you know anybody *that / whose* can translate this text into French?

9 Those are the men *whom / whose* children are my students.

10 Have you seen the box *what / that* I left here on the desk?

2 ▶ Match.

Ex.	*She's the woman*	a	when we met?
1	That's the hospital	b	who will take our case?
2	Is he the lawyer	c	where we stayed isn't there anymore.
3	They own a horse	d	*whose son won first prize.*
4	Do you remember the year	e	that has won several races.
5	Is he the doctor	f	whom I spoke yesterday.
6	The hotel	g	where you had your operation?
7	She's the manager to	h	where I had my operation.
8	Where's the hospital	i	who operated on your leg?

Defining Relative Clauses

We use defining relative clauses to give essential information about the person, animal or thing we are talking about. Without this information, we would not know what was being referred to. We don't use commas in this type of clause.
The man who/that was waiting on the corner was her brother.
The dog that/which was barking had been abandoned.

Notes

We can omit a relative pronoun when it is the object of a defining relative clause.
John is the one we hired last month. = *John is the one who/that we hired last month.*
These are the CDs Mary lent me. = *These are the CDs that/which Mary lent me.*

3 ▸ Choose the correct answer. (Note: " – " means "no relative pronoun.")

While my friend and I were going to the library yesterday, we met a man (Ex.) .... wanted to know where the nearest library was. We told him that the building (1) .... looked like a school was in fact the old library. He said he'd just been talking to someone (2) .... had told him that there wasn't a library in the town at all. We assured him that the person to (3) .... he had spoken was mistaken, and then we showed him the books (4) .... we were carrying and told him that we were going to the library, too. We walked together for a while, and the man explained the reason (5) .... he wanted to go to the library. He said that he had written a book and last Monday was the day (6) .... his book had been published. He wanted to go to the library to see if the book (7) .... he had written was there. We thought this was very exciting, as we'd never met anybody (8) .... book was actually in our local library. And it was even more exciting (9) .... we arrived at the library and found that our new friend's book was there. It was part of the display of new books (10) .... the librarian had arranged that very morning!

Ex.	**a** *which*	**b** *what*	**ⓒ** *who*
1	**a** what	**b** that	**c** where
2	**a** –	**b** who	**c** whom
3	**a** whose	**b** who	**c** whom
4	**a** what	**b** –	**c** where
5	**a** –	**b** what	**c** when
6	**a** when	**b** which	**c** whose
7	**a** what	**b** that	**c** whose
8	**a** –	**b** who	**c** whose
9	**a** what	**b** when	**c** –
10	**a** when	**b** which	**c** what

4 ▸ Complete the sentences using who/that or that/which only where necessary. Write " – " if no relative pronoun is needed.

Ex. *Shakespeare is one of the famous people ....who/that....... lived in Stratford-on-Avon.*

1 *Great Expectations is one of the best books .... I have ever read.*

2 *The information .... is contained in this instruction manual is difficult to understand.*

3 *The house .... we used to live in has been demolished.*

4 *Those are the people .... we met earlier today.*

5 *Have you seen the movie .... is all about the life of Iris Murdoch?*

6 *I have a lot of friends .... are interested in the environment.*

7 *The book .... I lent you is one of my favorites.*

8 *I'll never forget the ceremony .... we had when we graduated.*

Non-Defining Relative Clauses

➤ We use non-defining relative clauses to give extra information about the person, animal or thing in the main clause. The information is not essential to the meaning of the sentence.
➤ Non-defining clauses are separated from the rest of the sentence by commas.
➤ We use *who* (for people) and *which* (for things). *That* is not used in non-defining relative clauses.

My boss, who is very good at explaining things, has worked for the company for three years.
This book, which my sister gave me, is the best one I've read for a long time.

5 Underline the relative clauses in the sentences below. Then write D for defining clause and N for non-defining clause.

Ex. *This bag, <u>which I bought at an Italian market,</u> is made of goat skin.* __N__

1 The boy who was sitting next to me at the wedding is my nephew. _____
2 Tom, whose boat we were on, promised to teach us all about sailing. _____
3 He's the man whose boat we all went sailing on last weekend. _____
4 Our new car, which is Japanese, is better than our old one. _____
5 The furniture which is being delivered tomorrow was ordered from abroad. _____
6 This furniture, which was delivered yesterday, is made of Swedish pine. _____

6 Complete the second sentence with a relative clause so that it means the same as the first two sentences.

Ex. *Rose is our English teacher. She is planning a field trip to Washington, D.C.*
Our English teacher, ... whose name is Rose ...., is planning a field trip to Washington, D.C.

1 That's the professor. He gave most of his students low grades last year.
That's the professor ....

2 That's the place. We have to go there to vote.
That's the place ....

3 That building is called the Louvre. It's where the *Mona Lisa* can be seen.
That building, ..., is where the *Mona Lisa* can be seen.

4 The museum was built a hundred years ago. It is now being renovated.
The museum, ..., is now being renovated.

5 San Francisco is in northern California. My friends got married there.
San Francisco, ..., is in northern California.

6 That man went to the last Olympic Games. His son is a champion weightlifter.
That man, ..., went to the last Olympic Games.

Clauses of Result and Related Structures

➤ Clauses of result tell us the results of an action. They always come after the main clause and are introduced as follows:

so + subject + verb	*I was tired, so I went to bed early.*
so + adjective/adverb + (*that*) + subject + verb	*She works so hard that she got a raise.*
such + (*a/an*) adjective + noun + (*that*) + subject + verb	*It was such a bad storm that we stayed home.*

➤ Result can also be expressed in a main clause with these adverbs and prepositional phrases:

therefore	*I was tired. Therefore I went to bed early.*
consequently/as a consequence	*She works hard. Consequently, she got a raise.*
as a result	*Our oil supply is running out. As a result, scientists are searching for new forms of energy.*

Notes

We often use *such* and *so* with quantity expressions:
➤ *such a lot of* + plural/uncountable noun
They ate such a lot of burgers/food at lunch that they weren't hungry at dinnertime.
➤ *so much/little* + uncountable noun
There was so much rain that many villages flooded.
➤ *so many/few* + countable noun
I had so many books that I had to buy a second bookcase.

7 ▶ **Complete the sentences with the words from the box.**

consequently	few	little	many	of	result	so	such (x2)

Ex. It was ....*such*.......... a good movie that we went to see it again the following evening.

1 They worked hard all morning, and as a .... their boss gave them the afternoon off.

2 They have so .... money that they decided not to go on vacation this year.

3 He was extremely rude to the boss. ...., he was fired!

4 He made so .... mistakes that he had to retake the exam the following month.

5 I knew so .... people at the party that I wanted to leave after only half an hour.

6 The TV station received such a lot .... complaints that they decided to cancel the series.

7 They bought .... beautiful clothes that we all felt a little jealous.

8 I went to Paris last year, ... I was able to see the Eiffel Tower.

Clauses of Reason and Related Structures

➤ Clauses of reason explain why something happened. They can come before or after the main clause and are introduced as follows:

because + subject + verb	She stayed home because he wasn't feeling well.
as/since + subject + verb	As/Since the boss was ill, we canceled the meeting.
due to the fact that + subject + verb	He quit due to the fact that he didn't get along with the boss.
the reason (that) + subject + verb	We were curious to learn the reason (that) he had resigned.

➤ Reason can also be expressed in a main clause with these phrases:

because of + noun	He quit because of a disagreement with the boss.
due to + noun	They were delayed due to an accident on the bridge.
the reason for + noun	No one knew the reason for his resignation.

8 ▶ **Rewrite the sentences using the words in parentheses.**

Ex. He wore a scarf and gloves because it was snowing. (since)
     Since it was snowing, he wore a scarf and gloves.

1 My cousin never explained why he was in a bad mood yesterday. (reason for)

   ....

2 There was ice on the road, so we arrived home very late. (due to)

   ....

3 I didn't feel well, so I asked if I could leave work early. (because)

   ....

4 He was late for work because he had been stuck in traffic. (the reason)

   ....

5 It was foggy. I had to drive very slowly. (because of)

   ....

Clauses of Purpose and Related Structures

➤ Clauses of purpose explain why someone does something. They can come before or after the main clause and are introduced as follows:

so that + subject + verb   *He borrowed my car so that he could take his girlfriend out.*
in case + subject + verb   *I left early in case there was traffic.*

➤ When *so that* and *in case* express future purpose, we follow them with present tense verbs or imperatives.
I'll pay by credit card so that I don't need to carry a lot of cash.
In case I need to call you later, please take your cell phone.

➤ Purpose can also be expressed with these structures:

in order to + base form of verb   *I bought this book in order to learn about American history.*
to + base form of verb   *They went to the police station to confess the crime.*
for + noun/gerund   *He made that cupboard for towels and sheets.*

9 ▸ Join the sentences using the words in parentheses.

Ex. *They joined a gym. They wanted to get in shape. (to)*
They joined a gym to get in shape.

1 He called the police. He wanted to report a stolen car. (in order to)

....

2 I'll take an umbrella. It may rain later. (in case)

....

3 The director visited our office. He wanted to make sure everything was being done correctly. (to)

....

4 He went to the drugstore. He wanted some aspirin. (for)

....

5 They bought new clothes. They wanted to look good at the wedding. (in order to)

....

6 He gave me some money. I needed it to go shopping. (so that)

....

Clauses of Contrast and Concession and Related Structures

➤ Clauses of contrast and concession are used to introduce information that is different from or contrary to information in the main clause. They can come before or after the main clause and are introduced as follows:

but/yet + subject + verb   *He's kind, but/yet he sometimes loses his temper.*
although/even though + subject + verb   *Although/Even though it was raining, we went jogging.*
despite the fact that + subject + verb   *Despite the fact that he didn't feel well, he went to work.*
while/whereas + subject + verb   *Your boss isn't strict, whereas/while mine is.*

➤ Contrast and concession can also be expressed in a main clause as follows:

in spite of/despite + noun   *In spite of/Despite her illness, she never complains.*
however/nevertheless, + subject + verb   *He got into Harvard. However/Nevertheless, he's going to take a year off to travel.*

Notes

When a clause of concession or contrast comes before the main clause, we follow it with a comma.
When it comes after the main clause, we do not use a comma. (See examples above.)

However can come at the beginning or end of a sentence. When the subject is a noun (and not a pronoun), it can also come after the subject. It is always followed (and/or preceded) by a comma.
He's very intelligent. However, sometimes he's lazy./Sometimes he's lazy, however.
He's very intelligent. His grades, however, have fallen recently.

10 ▶ **Choose the correct answer.**

Ex.   He's seventy-five, (yet)/ despite he never seems to get tired.

1   Despite / In spite the weather, we enjoyed the picnic.

2   You can complain all you like. Although / However, I won't change my mind.

3   We walked all the way to the top of the mountain despite / even though it was a hard climb.

4   Your writing is neat, however / whereas mine is incredibly messy!

5   The actor wasn't feeling well, despite / but he went on stage and acted superbly.

6   I like you while / in spite of the fact that you boss me around.

7   Although / Yet I used do well in physics, I didn't do so well in chemistry.

8   I didn't have much experience. Even though / Nevertheless, the boss asked me to write several reports.

Clauses of Manner

Clauses of manner explain the way in which something happens. They are introduced by as if/as though.

As if/as though follow the verbs act, appear, be, behave, feel, look, seem, smell, sound, taste to show how someone or something behaves, feels, etc.
You look as though you need a rest.
It smells as if something's burning.

As if/as though follow other verbs to tell us how somebody does something.
He drives as if someone is chasing him.
You dance as though your feet are on fire.

We use as if/as though + past tense when we are talking about an imaginary situation in the present.
We usually use were instead of was for all forms.
He behaves as if he were the boss. (He isn't.)
You act as if you were an expert. (You aren't.)

Notes

We can use like to replace as if/as though in everyday speech.
It feels as if it's below freezing.
It feels like it's below freezing.

11 ▶ **Match.**

Ex.   He plays the violin as if   a   the temperature has fallen below freezing.

1   They sang as though   b   he were my boss.

2   You look as though   c   it was the funniest thing he'd ever heard.

3   It feels like   d   you have been crying.

4   She talked as if   e   he were a soloist with a symphony orchestra.

5   He laughed like   f   it's raining.

6   She looks as if   g   she knew all about metaphysics!

7   He acts as though   h   they were a professional group.

8   It sounds like   i   she's had bad news.

Pairwork

Work with a partner. Using clauses of reason, manner, contrast, purpose and result, start sentences and ask your partner to complete them. Say which kind of clause he or she must use. For example:

A: I'm going out now ... (clause of reason)
B: I'm going out now because I'm too hot in here.

Writing

Imagine a scene in the middle of a town or city on a busy Saturday morning. Describe the scene in as much detail as you can. Say who the people are in the scene, what they are doing, why they are doing it, how they are doing it, etc. Try to use a variety of relative clauses and other clauses and structures that you have studied in this unit.

1 ▶ Rewrite the sentences in reported speech.

Ex. *"Where were you at 6 o'clock?" she asked him.*
She asked him ....*where he had been at 6 o'clock*..

1 "The weather is awful today," he said.

He said ....

2 "The children are playing in the yard at the moment," he said.

He said ....

3 "Will you help me paint the kitchen, please?" he asked his cousin.

He asked his cousin ....

4 "We may go shopping tomorrow morning," they said.

They said ....

5 "Do you like using the Internet?" I asked him.

I asked him ....

6 "How old were you on your last birthday?" he asked me.

He asked me ....

2 ▶ Find the extra word in each sentence and write it on the dotted line.

Ex. *I asked the police for to come as quickly as they could.* ....*for*..........

1 The boss had asked us to work late before the previous day. ....

2 The builder warned me about not to touch the wet paint on the front door. ....

3 He asked the competitors to have wait for a few minutes. ....

4 Henry asked William to save some cake for him please. ....

5 The personal trainer refused her to let them use the gym on their own. ....

6 The doctor told me do not to eat too much sugar. ....

3 ▶ Rewrite the sentences in reported speech using the verbs in parentheses in the correct form.

Ex. *"Let's buy her a new CD," John said. (suggest)*
John ....*suggested buying / that they buy her a new CD.*..

1 "Don't forget to go to the dentist," he said to me. (remind)

He ....

2 "Shall I take the garbage out?" he said. (offer)

He ....

3 "Would you like to stay for dinner?" he asked them. (invite)

He ....

4 "I'm late because my car broke down," he told us. (explain)

He ....

5 "I'll pay for lunch today," my friend said. (insist)

My friend ....

6 "You're right; I did break your coffee cup," he said. (admit)

He ....

4 ▶ **Choose the correct answer.**

Ex.   ⟨Can you⟩/ *Are you able* run a marathon?

1   He hopes he *can* / *will be able to* speak Italian fluently by the end of the two-year course.

2   He *can* / *can to* drive a car.

3   *Do I need* / *Have I* to make the sandwiches right away?

4   You really *must* / *need* stop biting your nails.

5   We don't *have to* / *need* special equipment to go hiking. Just wear comfortable shoes.

6   I *had to* / *must* go to the dentist last week.

7   He *has* / *must* buy some food if he's going to have friends over for dinner.

8   She *must* / *could* play the piano very well when she was young.

5 ▶ **Complete the sentences with the words from the box.**

| asked | didn't (x2) | don't | have | need (x2) | needn't | to |

Ex.   You ....*don't*......... have to walk to work today. I can drive you there.

1   We .... need to bring a hair dryer as there was one in our hotel room.

2   Did you have .... pay extra for phone calls?

3   .... we stay here until 10 o'clock?

4   You .... buy the most expensive jeans you see. Try to find some cheaper ones.

5   They needn't .... worried about the storm. It wasn't as bad as they had predicted.

6   I .... need to buy milk as my roommate had already bought some.

7   She needn't have .... the waiter for water. He was going to bring it anyway.

8   Do I .... to wait for you until you finish work?

6 ▶ **Check (✓) the correct sentence.**

Ex.   *I can't stay out late because I have to get up early in the morning.* ✓
      I need stay out late because I have got to get up early in the morning. ____

1   May I have the afternoon off to go to my son's graduation? ____
    Must I have the afternoon off to go to my son's graduation? ____

2   May you lend me your calculator, please? ____
    Will you lend me your calculator, please? ____

3   The city is dangerous at night. You must not go out alone. ____
    The city is dangerous at night. You don't have to go out alone. ____

4   You can't take photos in the museum. ____
    You don't take photos in the museum. ____

5   Will I change the date of my hotel reservation, please? ____
    Could I change the date of my hotel reservation, please? ____

6   It was kind of you to buy me flowers, but you needn't have. ____
    It was kind of you to buy me flowers, but you need not. ____

7 ▶ **Choose the correct answer.**

Ex. *We couldn't have afforded this house if it .... any more expensive than it was.*
  a *was being*   **ⓑ** *had been*   **c** *were*

1 I .... for more time to finish my report if I had known how difficult it was going to be to write.
  a would ask   **b** have asked   **c** would have asked

2 He usually turns the photocopier on if he .... to work first.
  a will get   **b** is getting   **c** gets

3 She .... it if you tell her what the others are saying about her!
  a not like   **b** won't like   **c** don't like

4 If Harriet gets home before I do, ... you .... her that I'll be late, please?
  a can, tell   **b** will, be telling   **c** can, say

5 She wouldn't have gone to the party last night if she .... her ex-boyfriend had been invited.
  a knew   **b** has known   **c** had known

6 If I .... my credit cards, I would tell the police immediately.
  a have lost   **b** lose   **c** lost

8 ▶ **Complete the sentences with the correct form of the verbs in parentheses.**

Ex. *If you don't explain clearly, I .... won't understand .... what to do. (not understand)*

1 They .... to the movies if they had known the show was sold out. (not go)

2 If I .... you, I'd go home and go straight to bed; you look really tired. (be)

3 He .... on time if he had taken the express train. (arrive)

4 If I .... her, she would have bought bread on the way home. (remind)

5 Men will not be allowed into the restaurant if they .... a tie. (not wear)

6 If he .... this mess, he will be furious! (see)

7 I'll tell you what happened as long as you .... anybody else. (not tell)

8 He .... surgery if the doctor had diagnosed his problem sooner. (not need)

9 ▶ **Rewrite the sentences using the words given. Use between two and five words.**

Ex. *If you stop smoking, your cough will get better.* **won't**
  Your cough .... won't get better .... if you don't stop smoking.

1 Unless you work harder, you will not get promoted. **long**
  As ...., you will get promoted.

2 He went to prison because he had committed a serious crime. **not**
  He .... to prison if he hadn't committed a serious crime.

3 I'm asking you to lend me money because I haven't got any. **had**
  If ...., I wouldn't be asking you to lend me some.

4 If you don't feel good about it, don't go to the wedding alone. **unless**
  Don't go to the wedding alone .... about it.

5 I didn't know about the concert or I would have gone. **known**
  If .... the concert, I would have gone.

6 In your position, I think I'd try to find a new apartment. **were**
  If .... try to find a new apartment.

10 Complete the second sentence with a relative clause so that it means the same as the first two sentences.

Ex. *The cookbook is very old and worth a lot of money. It is stored in a box in the attic.*
The cookbook, ...which is stored in a box in the attic.........., is very old and worth a lot of money.

1 Chloe helps my mom with the cleaning. She lives in the same street as us.
Chloe, ..., helps my mom with the cleaning.

2 Our neighbor's son won an Olympic medal. He is a wrestler.
Our neighbor's son, ..., won an Olympic medal.

3 A girl has just sent me an e-mail. I used to go to school with her.
A girl .... has just sent me an e-mail.

4 Thomas takes his horses all over the country. His horses have won lots of prizes.
Thomas, ..., takes them all over the country.

5 He was accused of setting fire to the school. I used to be a student there.
He was accused of setting fire to the school ....

6 Have you seen the jacket? I left it on the chair in the kitchen.
Have you seen the jacket ....?

11 Choose the correct answer.

Ex. *He was such a kind man such /(that) everybody admired him.*

1 They didn't come to the meeting *because / due to* the fact that they all had the flu.
2 I had learned *so less / so few* of my lines that I asked someone else to take over my part in the play.
3 *Despite / In spite* of his problems, he offered to stay with his friend and look after him until he had recovered.
4 It looks to me *as if / though* it's going to be a cold and windy weekend again.
5 I saved my money *so that / in order to* be able to afford to buy a nice birthday present for my sister.
6 He was driving after having worked for fifteen hours. *However, / Therefore*, it's not surprising that he had an accident.
7 He is unfriendly and impatient, *whereas / despite* his brother is completely the opposite.
8 We prepared all the food for the dinner, *but / even though* we had never cooked anything before!

12 Find the mistakes and rewrite the sentences correctly.

Ex. *He looks to as if he is going to faint.*
He looks as if he is going to faint....

1 We invited lots of people to our play. Although, a lot of them didn't come.
....

2 You're working too hard and, as a consequently, your health is beginning to suffer.
....

3 Despite of the fact that it was cold, my friends went swimming.
....

4 I fixed the bike that my brother would be able to ride it.
....

5 My friend likes beach vacations, when I prefer hiking in the mountains.
....

6 I stayed up late last night because of I didn't have to go to work today.
....

Count and Noncount Nouns

Count Nouns
Most nouns are count nouns and they have a singular and a plural form.

watch	➜ watches	toy	➜ toys	baby	➜ babies
dress	➜ dresses	knife	➜ knives	foot	➜ feet

Noncount Nouns
There are also noncount nouns, which do not have a plural form. When a noncount noun is the subject of a sentence, we use it with a verb in the third person singular.

➤ Food: *rice, spaghetti, sugar, cheese, salt, pepper, flour, butter, bread, meat*.
➤ Liquids: *water, coffee, tea, lemonade, oil, milk*.
➤ Materials: *wood, glass, pottery, china, silk, plastic, leather*.
➤ Abstract nouns: *knowledge, love, freedom, justice, anger, beauty, fear, education*.
➤ Other nouns: *information, luggage, baggage, advice, behavior, garbage, trash, litter, news, accommodation, weather, furniture*.

We don't put *a* or *an* in front of noncount nouns or plural count nouns. We can use *some* in affirmative sentences and *any* in questions and negative sentences.
We must get some advice about this.   *He left some books on the table.*
Is there any milk left?   *Are there any oranges on that tree?*
They don't have any furniture yet.   *I couldn't see any ships on the horizon.*

When we offer or ask for something, we use *some*, not *any*.
Would you like some food?
Can I have some water?

We can make noncount nouns countable by using phrases of quantity like *a bag of, a jar of, a pack of*.
The baker ordered two big bags of flour.
I bought a jar of peanut butter today.
There's a pack of gum on the table.
We need three loaves of bread for the party.

Notes

When we order food or drinks, we sometimes use *a/an, one/two*, etc., with noncount nouns.
Can we have three coffees and two teas, please?

1 ▶ Complete the sentences with a, an, some or any.

Ex.   Can I borrow ....*a*............ pencil, please?

1   Would you like .... coffee with your cake?

2   Can I borrow .... cup of sugar?

3   Unfortunately, there isn't .... milk left.

4   Jane bought me .... vase for my birthday.

5   Do you have .... brothers or sisters?

6   We saw .... ducks in the pond.

7   Is there .... teacher in your family?

8   He is .... actor, I think.

2 ▶ Check (✓) the correct sentence.

Ex.   Does she have any brothers? ___✓___
       Does she have a brothers? _____

1   Can I have three slices of cheese, please? _____
     Can I have three slices of cheeses, please? _____

2   I want some informations about flight times. _____
     I want some information about flight times. _____

3   Coffee aren't very good for you. _____
     Coffee isn't very good for you. _____

4   Can I have some salad with my chicken, please? _____
     Can I have any salad with my chicken, please? _____

5   I bought some loaves of breads. _____
     I bought some loaves of bread. _____

6   Two coffee, please. _____
     Two coffees, please. _____

7   Do you have some luggage? _____
     Do you have any luggage? _____

8   What's the good news? _____
     What are the good news? _____

Nouns That Are Both Count and Noncount Nouns

Certain nouns can be used as either count or noncount nouns, but there is a difference in meaning:

	Count	Noncount
➤ glass	I want a glass of milk. (a drinking container) I want two glasses of milk.	There is some broken glass on the road. (the material)
➤ paper	I'm going to buy a paper. (newspaper) We get two papers delivered on Sundays.	I need some paper to write on. (a sheet of paper)
➤ iron	We have bought a new iron. (for clothes) We have bought two new irons this year.	The gate is made of iron. (the metal)
➤ chocolate	Thank you for the box of chocolates. (individual pieces of chocolate candy)	This cake is made with flour, butter, eggs, sugar and chocolate. (the substance)
➤ hair	There is a hair in my soup. (a single strand) There are some hairs in my soup!	Comb your hair before you go out. (all the hair on your head)
➤ room	Can I see your spare room? (part of a house) How many rooms are there in your new house?	There isn't any room for a piano in my house. (space)
➤ business	My father owns a small business. (company) Small businesses have to fight to succeed.	Business has been slow lately. (commercial activity)

3 ► **Choose the correct answer.**

Ex.   *You don't need much* (chocolate) / *chocolates to make this cake.*

1   Your *hairs / hair* looks lovely today.

2   How many *rooms / room* are there in your house?

3   Can I have *any / a* glass of milk?

4   How *much / many* paper do I need for the report?

5   I'd like two *coffee / coffees*, please.

6   There really isn't *rooms / room* for a new bookcase in your bedroom.

7   I thought you had bought *some / a* new luggage.

8   Those railings are made of *irons / iron*.

9   My brother started *a / some* small business last year.

10   Mary's father hasn't got much *hair / hairs* on his head. He's almost bald.

Masculine and Feminine Forms

Some nouns have different masculine and feminine forms. Some of these are:

nephew – niece	*waiter – waitress*	*duke – duchess*
bridegroom – bride	*prince – princess*	*widower – widow*

Singular or Plural Verb Forms?

We use singular verbs with nouns that refer to:

➤ subjects.
   mathematics, physics, economics, politics
   Mathematics is my favorite subject and physics is my least favorite.

➤ illnesses.
   measles, mumps, tuberculosis
   Mumps is a common childhood disease.

➤ games.
   darts, billiards, dominoes
   Billiards is played in many countries.

➤ sports.
   athletics, gymnastics
   Gymnastics is interesting to watch.

➤ money, time periods, distance, weight.
   Thirty years is a long time to do the same job.
   A thousand dollars is a lot of money.

➤ groups of people when we are talking about them as a single unit.
   The government is deciding what to do.
   My son's class is planning an excursion to New York City.
   My family is important to me.
   My football team is doing well.

We use plural verb forms for nouns that describe objects with two parts, like *glasses*, *pants*, *pajamas*, *gloves*, *shorts*.
Where are my blue pants?
These scissors are only for paper.

We don't use *a* or *an* with these words, but we can use the phrase *a pair of ...* to refer to one item.
He bought a new pair of sunglasses last week.

4 ▸ **Complete the sentences with the correct form of the verb to be.**

Ex. *This pair of jeans .....is..... too small for me now.*

1 Dominoes .... a very old game.
2 Ten years .... a long time to go without visiting friends and family in your hometown.
3 Economics and physics .... my favorite subjects.
4 What .... the government going to do about the rising crime rate?
5 The pajamas I wanted .... too expensive.
6 Three thousand dollars .... a lot of money to pay for two nights in a hotel!
7 Measles .... a common childhood illness.
8 She's a good all-around athlete, but gymnastics .... what she's best at.

Articles

The Indefinite Article – *a / an*

The indefinite article is used with:

➤ singular count nouns when they are mentioned for the first time.
   I'd love to have a new car.
➤ certain numbers instead of *one*, and some quantifying phrases.
   a thousand   four times a month
   a million   once an hour
   twice a week $3 a pound
➤ singular count nouns when we are talking generally.
   I must buy a coat.
➤ nouns referring to jobs, nationality, religion or political beliefs.
   She's a biologist.
   He's an American.

Notes

We can use *per* instead of *a/an* in quantifying phrases.
The speed limit here is 30 miles an/per hour.
Chicken costs $2.50 a/per pound.

When a word begins with a vowel, but the vowel sounds like a consonant in the word, we use *a*.
Angela is a university graduate.

When a word begins with a consonant, but the consonant sounds like a vowel in the word, we use *an*.
I'll meet you in an hour.
The movie is about an FBI agent.

The indefinite article is not used with:

➤ plural count nouns or noncount nouns.
   Apples are good for you.
   What delicious cheese!
➤ adjectives that are not followed by a noun.
   He's handsome.
➤ names of meals (unless there is an adjective before them).
   Let's make breakfast now.
   We had a late lunch, so we didn't eat dinner.

5 ▸ **Complete the sentences with a, an or –.**

Ex. *I thought you were ......an.... honest person!*

1 You're wearing .... unusual pair of glasses today.
2 What .... delicious cheese!
3 The babysitter charges $10 .... hour.
4 There isn't .... European capital city that I haven't visited.
5 Have you made .... progress with your job applications?
6 There's nothing like .... nice tall glass of iced tea on .... hot summer day.
7 Don't drive the wrong way down .... one-way street!
8 We go to karate classes twice .... week.

Articles

The Definite Article – *the*

The definite article is used:

➤ with singular and plural count nouns and with noncount nouns.
The frying pan is on the stove.
The cats are chasing the birds.
The cheese is moldy.

➤ when we refer back to something or someone we have already mentioned in the previous sentence.
He sent me some flowers. The flowers were beautiful.

➤ when we are talking about someone or something specific.
The scarf I'm wearing was knitted by my best friend.

➤ with nouns which are regarded as being unique.
The moon shines at night.

➤ with musical instruments *(the piano, the drums)* and names of dances *(the samba, the twist).*

➤ with historical periods *(the Ice Age)* or events *(the Second World War).*

➤ with groups of islands *(the Philippines)* and countries with common nouns in their names *(the United Kingdom, the Czech Republic, the United States).*

➤ with names of rivers *(the Nile)*, seas *(the Dead Sea)*, mountain ranges *(the Rockies, the Andes)*, oceans *(the Atlantic)*, and deserts *(the Gobi Desert).*

➤ with names of hotels *(the Hilton)*, theaters *(the Apollo)*, museums *(the Natural History Museum)*, art galleries *(the National Gallery)*, ships *(the Queen Elizabeth)*, newspapers *(The Times)* and organizations *(the United Nations).*

➤ with the plural form of a last name, to refer to two or more people in a family *(the Clarks, the Smiths).*

➤ with official titles (without the name).
The mayor is visiting our area.

➤ with superlatives.
That was the best meal I've ever had!

➤ with ordinal numbers and the words *only* and *last*.
That was the first time I'd ever seen a lion.
He was the only person who really understood her.

➤ with dates, and with the words *morning*, *afternoon* and *evening*.
His birthday is the 29th of March. (We can also say "March 29th.")
I'll see you in the morning.

➤ with the words *station, theater, library, city, village,* etc.
They went to the theater.

➤ with adjectives referring to a group of people *(the homeless, the deaf, the Japanese, the French).*

The definite article is not used:

➤ with plural count nouns and noncount nouns when they are used generally.
Tigers eat other animals.

➤ with names of cities *(Rome)*, roads *(Park Street)*, parks *(Yellowstone Park)*, stations *(New Street Station).*

➤ with most countries *(Brazil)*, mountains *(Mount Fuji)*, islands *(Jersey)*, continents *(Asia)*, lakes *(Lake Michigan).*

➤ with abstract nouns.
Jealousy is not a pleasant emotion.

➤ with the words *school, bed, prison, college, university, court,* or *home* when they are used as a general term.
Shh! The children are in bed. (They're sleeping.)
Their son is in college now. (He's a student.)
The use of *the* before these words means the speaker is referring to a specific place.
Your shoes are under the bed.
The college has an excellent music department.

➤ with people's names, or with people's titles when their names are mentioned, too.
Her name is Mandy.
Look! Is that Mayor Jones over there?

➤ with the names of sports, games, hobbies, days, months, celebrations, colors, drinks and meals.
We like basketball.
I'll meet you next Saturday.
Labor Day is next week.
Would you like tea or coffee?

➤ with names made up of two words when the first word is the name of a person or place.
I'll meet you at Sam's Diner at 9 o'clock.
The flight has been diverted to Kennedy Airport.

➤ with the names of languages without the word *language*.
My mom is learning Russian.
The Chinese language has many dialects.

6 Complete the sentences with *the* or –.

Ex. *We had a great time when we went to .... Lake Ontario.*

1   He's always .... first person to arrive at work.
2   Their house has a beautiful view of .... Hudson River.
3   My brother really enjoys .... coffee after dinner.
4   Have you ever been to .... United States?
5   What is the government doing to help .... homeless?
6   I didn't know you played .... badminton.
7   Let's meet outside .... library at 10 o'clock.
8   Who was .... first president of .... United States?
9   Will the bank robber be sent to .... prison?
10   I've got tickets for the musical at .... Sheridan Theater.

One / Ones

We use *one* in the singular and *ones* in the plural to avoid repeating a previously mentioned noun.
He doesn't drive a red car. He drives a black one.
Your new glasses are much nicer than your old ones.

When there is an adjective before *one*, we use *the* (for a specific noun) or *an/an* or *any* (for something indefinite).
She didn't buy a new dress. She wore the one she bought for her brother's wedding last year.
They live in an old house, not a new one.

We use *one* to talk about one person or thing or a number of people or things.
One shop sold computers and the other one sold DVD players.
One of my best friends went to Harvard University.

7 Complete the sentences with *a, an, one* or *ones.*

Ex. *Jenny borrowed his Beatles CD and I borrowed his Santana ....one........ .*

1   The red chairs are too small, but the blue .... are just the right size. Let's buy them.
2   This is .... interesting article about global warming.
3   Your living room is too small for such a large sofa. .... smaller one would be better.
4   I can't decide which dress I like best. Which .... would you buy?
5   Take a look at the photographs and tell me which .... you want copies of.
6   .... of my friends is going to the Picasso exhibition.

8 Find the extra word in each sentence and write it on the dotted line.

Ex. *My son studies the economics at a small college in Vermont. ....the..........*

1   I love those black shoes, but I didn't like them the brown ones. ....
2   Our flight leaves from the Kennedy Airport at 10 o'clock. ....
3   The one government of the USA is changing some of its tax laws again. ....
4   I believe violent criminals should spend a long time in the prison. ....
5   He's in the bed because he has a bad cold. ....
6   This is my sister, the Julie. ....
7   We have fish at least once for a week. ....
8   Was your grandfather one a doctor at the local hospital? ....
9   He was the first person in his family to graduate a college. ....
10   They went to the hospital to visit a one friend. ....

Quantifiers – Much / Many / A Lot Of / Lots Of

We use *much* (+ noncount noun) and *many* (+ plural count noun) in negative sentences and questions.
There wasn't much time so they went by taxi.
Does he have much money?
There aren't many parks in this town.
Does your company employ many people?

We use *a lot of / lots of* with noncount nouns and plural count nouns. They are usually used in affirmative sentences.
There's a lot of food left over.
She has lots of cousins.

Notes

We use *too much* and *too many* to talk about a quantity that is more than we need or want.
This coffee has too much sugar in it. I can't drink it.
I don't like going to places where there are too many people.

So, too, very, how and *as* are often used before *much* and *many*.
I want that dress so much.
He's had too much sun.
Thank you very much for your help.
Do you know how much time you've wasted?
Take as many cookies as you want.

Quantifiers – A Few / Few / A Little / Little

We use *a few, few, a little* and *little* to talk about small quantities. When the quantity is sufficient, we use *a few* and *a little*. When the quantity isn't sufficient, we use *few* and *little*.

We use *a few* and *few* with plural count nouns.
He gave me a few ideas for my report.
There are few movies that I've enjoyed more than this one.

Notes

We use *a little* and *little* with noncount nouns.
She needs a little help with her work.
There's little plant life in the desert.

We can put *very* in front of *few* and *little*.
He told very few people about his first marriage.
She gained very little by behaving like that.

9 ▸ Choose the correct answer.

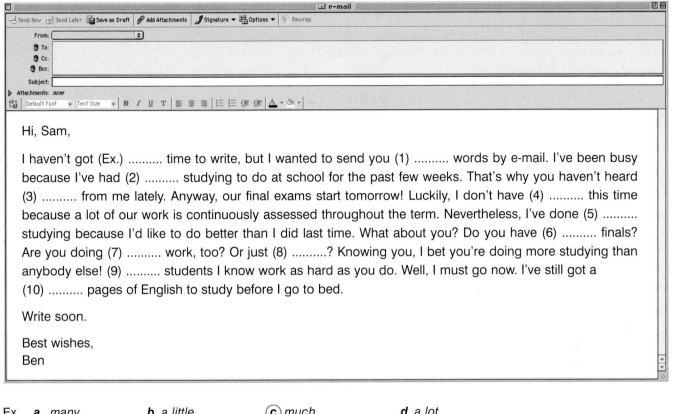

Hi, Sam,

I haven't got (Ex.) .... time to write, but I wanted to send you (1) .... words by e-mail. I've been busy because I've had (2) .... studying to do at school for the past few weeks. That's why you haven't heard (3) .... from me lately. Anyway, our final exams start tomorrow! Luckily, I don't have (4) .... this time because a lot of our work is continuously assessed throughout the term. Nevertheless, I've done (5) .... studying because I'd like to do better than I did last time. What about you? Do you have (6) .... finals? Are you doing (7) .... work, too? Or just (8) ....? Knowing you, I bet you're doing more studying than anybody else! (9) .... students I know work as hard as you do. Well, I must go now. I've still got a (10) .... pages of English to study before I go to bed.

Write soon.

Best wishes,
Ben

Ex.	**a** *many*	**b** *a little*	**ⓒ** *much*	**d** *a lot*
1	**a** a little	**b** a few	**c** much	**d** many
2	**a** much	**b** many	**c** a lot of	**d** a few
3	**a** many	**b** a few	**c** a little	**d** much
4	**a** much	**b** many	**c** a few	**d** a lot of
5	**a** a lot	**b** a few	**c** lots of	**d** much
6	**a** much	**b** many	**c** a lot	**d** a little
7	**a** a little	**b** a lot of	**c** many	**d** a few
8	**a** a lot of	**b** a few	**c** a little	**d** much
9	**a** Much	**b** Few	**c** Many	**d** A little
10	**a** many	**b** much	**c** few	**d** lots of

Both / Either / Neither

We use *both*, *either* and *neither* to talk about two people or things.

Both / Both of is used in the affirmative and requires a plural verb.
(Becky is tired. Sue is tired.)
Both Becky and Sue are tired.
Both girls are tired. = Both of the girls are tired.
Both of them are tired.

Either is followed by a singular count noun and requires a singular verb.
You can buy the red one or the blue one. Either shirt is fine by me.

Either of is followed by a plural count noun and is usually followed by a singular verb.
Either of those shirts is fine by me.

Neither is followed by a singular count noun and has a negative meaning. It is followed by a singular verb.
Neither girl is going to college.

Neither of is followed by a plural count noun and is usually followed by a singular verb.
Neither of my sisters is going to college.

Neither ... nor and *either ... or* can be used with singular or plural verbs, depending on whether the subject that follows *nor* or *or* is singular or plural.
Neither Greg nor Rosemary eats meat.
Either my sister or your parents are going to babysit tomorrow.

All / None Of / Whole

We use *all / all of* and *none of* to talk about more than two people or things. *All* is plural, but *none* is considered singular in formal English.
All the new workers are doing well. = All of the new workers are doing well.
All of them are doing well.
None of my friends lives in the city.
None of them lives in the city.

Whole is followed by a singular count noun. We use *a/my/the/this + whole + noun.*
The baby was so tired that she slept for the whole night.

Notes

We can use *all* or *all of* instead of *whole.*
It has the same meaning, but the word order changes.
All the family / All of the family went out for the evening.
The whole family went out for the evening.

---

10 ▶ Check (✓) the two correct sentences.

Ex. *I love you very much.* ✓
     I love you many much. ____
     I love you so much. ✓

1   There is a lot of information on this website. ____
    There's many information on this website. ____
    Is there much information on this website? ____

2   Either of these jackets would suit you. ____
    You could wear either of these jackets. ____
    Do you like either this jacket nor that jacket? ____

3   Neither Mary nor Jane is going to the conference. ____
    Neither Mary nor Jane will be at the conference. ____
    Neither Mary or Jane were at the conference. ____

4   The all family went on vacation. ____
    All the family went on vacation. ____
    The whole family went on vacation. ____

5   They gave us lots of information. ____
    They gave us a lot of information. ____
    They gave us much information. ____

6   Both David and John plays tennis. ____
    Both David and John are tennis players. ____
    Both David and John play tennis. ____

11 ▶ Complete the sentences with the words from the box.

all	either	few	much	neither	nor	or	too	whole

Ex. *We might go to ....either........ Boston or New York for the long weekend.*

1   Neither my sister .... I wants to go to graduate school.
2   The .... team was awarded a prize for winning the tournament.
3   .... of the two women passed their driving test. They'll both have to take it again.
4   You can either stay at home .... come to the movies with us.
5   A .... of them are thinking about going to college in the USA.
6   .... members of the drama group are expected to come to tonight's rehearsal.
7   I'm surprised at how .... you have progressed this year.
8   There's just .... much grammar to learn!

Pairwork

Work with a partner. Take turns and tell each other all about the house or apartment you live in. Describe what is in each room. Try to use as many of the words you have learned in this unit as you can. For example:

In the kitchen there is a table and a few cupboards. They are all made of wood. There aren't many ... .

Writing

Imagine you are at the check-out counter at the supermarket and have just done your shopping for the week. Describe what is in your shopping cart. Try to make it as interesting as you can! For example:

There are three boxes of breakfast cereal. One of them has chocolate in it and one of them has almonds and bananas in it. There's some cheese and a lot of bread, because we all eat bread every day.
I also have some ... .

Present/Future Possibility

We use *could/may/might* + base form of verb to talk about things that are possible in the present or the future.
For ongoing activity, we use the continuous form: *could/may/might + be + -ing.*

Simple
He's not at work today. He could be sick.
He may not like the movie we saw.
She might go to the theater this evening, but
she's not sure.

Continuous
He feels awful. He could be coming down with the flu.
He's not in his room. He may be cutting the grass.
We might be going to the movies this evening.

Past Possibility

We use *could/may/might + have* + past participle to talk about things that were possible in the past when the speaker is not 100% sure. For ongoing activity, we use the continuous form: *could/may/might + have + been + -ing.*

Simple
Mark could have won the marathon.
They may have gone home already. I'll ask.
She might not have enjoyed the play.

Continuous
They could have been trying to call, but we weren't home.
Her eyes were all red. She may have been crying.
He had an accident. He might not have been driving
slowly enough.

We can use *could/might + have* + past participle to talk about things that were possible in the past but that didn't happen. (*May have* + past participle means something was possible, but we're not sure if it happened or not.)
He could have broken his leg in the fall, but luckily he was OK.
Your son might have hurt himself with that knife. You were lucky I saw him.

Notes

Could is not used in the negative to talk about possibility.

We can use *can* in affirmative sentences for possibility in the present when we are talking about something that is possible in theory. For specific situations in the present, we use *could, may* or *might.*
You can get snowed in if you live in that village. (It happens every few years.)
He could/may/might be stuck in traffic. (He should be home by now, but he isn't.)

1 ▸ **Check (✓) the correct sentence.**

Ex. *Jerry might be coming with us later on.* __✓__
     Jerry may have come with us later on. _____

1   Ian might have called while we were out. _____
    Ian could be called while we were out. _____

2   They could not buy new furniture next summer. _____
    They might not buy new furniture next summer. _____

3   This restaurant can get very busy on Saturday nights. _____
    This restaurant could have gotten very busy on Saturday nights. _____

4   She was lucky. She could have been hurt. _____
    She was lucky. She may have been hurt. _____

5   I didn't see Tom at the party. Sue may have forgotten to invite him. _____
    I didn't see Tom at the party. Sue could be forgetting to invite him. _____

6   You may be right. _____
    You may be being right. _____

2 ▸ **Complete the sentences with the correct form of the verbs in parentheses.**

Ex. *I haven't seen your book. Your brother might* .... *have borrowed* .... *it. (borrow)*

1   The police said poor road conditions could .... the accident. (cause)
2   We're still out of milk. Mom might .... shopping yet. (not go)
3   I might .... tired when I get home this evening because I'm going to work late. (be)
4   My keys are missing. Someone may .... them. (steal)
5   The doctor says I might .... allergic to pollen. (be)
6   They're lucky to be alive! Their house could .... during the earthquake. (fall down)
7   The weather forecast said it may .... tomorrow. (rain)
8   We may .... to the movies this evening. Do you want to come? (go)
9   The volcano could .... the whole town if it erupts. (destroy)
10 Lucy may .... to the meeting on Friday. (not come)

3 ▸ **Complete the sentences in your own words.**

Ex. *My brother isn't home yet. He may* ...*have gone to his friend's house.*...................................

1   Our English class was canceled today. Our teacher might ....
2   Our cat hasn't been home for three days. It may ....
3   He has bruises all over his body. He could ....
4   She can't find her purse. Someone might ....
5   That little girl is crying. She may ....
6   The red sports car is badly damaged. It might ....

Deduction – Must / Can't / Couldn't

We use *must* when we are sure something is true. *Must* is followed by the base form of the verb to talk about the present or the future, and by *have* + past participle to talk about the past. We can also use continuous forms: *must be* + *-ing* for present/future and *must have been* + *-ing* for the past.
The lights aren't on. He must be asleep.
She hasn't called, so she must still be on the plane.
I'm sorry. I must have forgotten to give you my address.
It's 10 o'clock. You must have been waiting for ages!

We use *can't* and *couldn't* when we are sure something is not true. *Can't* and *couldn't* are followed by the base form to talk about the present or the future, and by *have* + past participle to talk about the past. We can also use continuous forms: *can't/couldn't* + *be* + *-ing* and *can't/couldn't have* + *been* + past participle.
He can't be on vacation. I saw him an hour ago.
You couldn't eat five pizzas. You'd be ill!
She can't have introduced you to her brother; she hasn't got one.
It couldn't have been me you saw in town yesterday. I was in Boston.

4 Complete the sentences with must or can't/couldn't.

Ex. *He didn't answer the phone. He ....must.......... have been out.*

1   Melanie is in Australia, so you .... have seen her at work yesterday.
2   The professor has taught at Harvard for twenty years. He .... be at least 50 years old.
3   That .... be Jane's twin sister. They look identical.
4   He only played in the first half, so he .... have scored a goal near the end of the game.
5   He .... have bought a new bike because I haven't seen him riding that one before.
6   She .... be the new secretary. She works in the coffee shop down the street.

5 Write the words in the correct order.

Ex. *Jim / this / it / been / you / must / morning / have / saw*
     It must have been Jim you saw this morning.

1   they / money / spent / have / can't / their / all
    ....
2   you / your / yet / test / can't / driving / passed / have
    ....
3   been / she / very / the / heard / must / news / when / upset / have / she
    ....
4   he's / Peter / Brazil / to / have / couldn't / photo / taken / that / because / never / been
    ....
5   what / manager / can't / asked / you / have / you / the / understood
    ....

6 Match.

Ex. *Susan must be getting married*   a   because I saw her buying lots of new clothes.
1   James can't be manager of that bank   b   because I saw him working at the post office.
2   Lucy might have gotten a raise   c   because I saw the boss yelling at him again.
3   Anthony could be moving   d   *because I saw her trying on wedding dresses.*
4   Norman must have done something wrong   e   because I saw her at the doctor this morning.
5   Julia could be sick   f   because his rent's going up again.

7 ▶ Find the extra word in each sentence and write it on the dotted line.

Ex. *I think he may have done missed the bus.* ....*done*.........

1 He could have been helped me but he didn't want to. ....

2 He could might not be late this evening. ....

3 You could stay for an extra week if you might want to. ....

4 Drive carefully because the roads they may be slippery after the rain.

  ....

5 You can't have not finished all that work so soon! ....

6 The fog must have been caused their flight to be delayed. ....

7 Be careful because the glass might not break if you lean on it. ....

8 You must have be driven quickly to get here at this time. ....

9 When he could finds the report, he will start preparing for the meeting. ....

10 The students couldn't have done so badly on their finals. They must worked really hard all term. ....

8 ▶ Choose the correct answer.

Ex. *The report was due on Monday, so they* (must)*/ couldn't have worked all weekend to finish it.*

1 He *must / can't* have worked hard to get such a good raise.

2 She's so tall that she *can't / could* be a basketball player.

3 It *mustn't / can't* be snowing again!

4 He *may / could* not get a promotion after all.

5 You *must / could* be exhausted after all your hard work!

6 Pandas *can't / may* become extinct one day.

7 You *might / can* find this book useful for your report.

8 They aren't here. They *must / can* have gone home.

9 ▶ Rewrite the sentences using the words given. Use between two and five words.

Ex. *It's possible that they will buy a new apartment.* **may**
  They ....*may buy*................. *a new apartment.*

1 I'm sure he lied to me. **must**
  He .... to me.

2 I'm thinking of seeing that movie again this weekend. **might**
  I .... this weekend.

3 I'm sure he didn't write that e-mail himself. **can't**
  He .... that e-mail himself.

4 Perhaps the professor is busy in his office at the moment. **may**
  The professor .... in his office at the moment.

5 It's not possible that he's downloaded all the programs already. **can't**
  He .... the programs already.

6 I really don't think he has lost all the money he saved. **couldn't**
  He .... all the money he saved.

7 Perhaps the tree was damaged by the hurricane. **could**
  The tree .... the hurricane.

8 It's not possible that she's speaking Japanese. **can't**
  She .... Japanese.

10 ▶ **Choose the correct answer.**

Ex. *He .... be an expert sailor to have survived that terrible storm.*

    a *can't*   **(b)** *must*   **c** *couldn't*   **d** *may*

1   That Ford .... be Bob's car. He drives a Honda.

    a can't   **b** must   **c** could   **d** may

2   She .... have practiced for years to have become such a skilled ballet dancer.

    a can't   **b** could   **c** may   **d** must

3   We .... have met before because I don't remember you at all.

    a couldn't   **b** must   **c** may   **d** could

4   I'm not sure but I think he .... be the man I saw in the supermarket.

    a must   **b** may   **c** couldn't   **d** can't

5   I .... agree to help you, but you must give me more information first.

    a may   **b** can't   **c** couldn't   **d** mustn't

6   We were lucky. The fire .... have caused much more damage than it did.

    a can't   **b** must   **c** could   **d** can

7   It's quiet in the classroom. The lesson .... have started.

    a couldn't   **b** must   **c** mustn't   **d** can

8   We .... spend next weekend at home, but we aren't sure yet.

    a might   **b** must   **c** couldn't   **d** can't

11 ▶ **Complete the text by writing one word in each blank. More than one answer is possible.**

Look at that group of young people standing over there! I think they (Ex.) ....*may/might*............ have done something bad. They (1) .... have stolen something expensive from one of the stores. They (2) .... be feeling a bit guilty because they won't look at me. And they have a big bag with something in it that looks as if it (3) .... be a laptop. When I first saw them, I thought the boy with the black hair was my neighbor's son. Then I realized it (4) .... be him because he's on vacation in Mexico this week. I'm sure the tall boy has been in trouble before. He (5) .... be well known to the police. In fact, I (6) .... go down to the police station right now and talk to them. They (7) .... be interested to hear what a retired police officer has to say!

Pairwork

Work with a partner. Take turns thinking of situations and ask your partner to make deductions about them or to suggest possibilities about them. For example:

Student A: *The house is empty and all the lights are out.*
Student B: *The family must be out. They may be away on vacation. They might have gone to the movies.*

Student B: *Ron isn't home yet.*
Student A: *He may be working late. He can't have had an accident because he just called.*

Writing

Imagine you are a detective and you are at a crime scene investigating a burglary. You find the following: one window is smashed; the drawers are all open and things are hanging out of them; there is some blood on the floor; the TV and video are missing; there are large muddy footprints in the living room; there are two empty bottles of water on the table; the computer is on.

Write a report about what may/must/could/can't have happened. Use the language you have learned in this unit.

COULD YOU STOP WORKING SO HARD, PLEASE? YOU'RE MAKING THE REST OF US LOOK BAD.

Gerunds

Gerunds are nouns. To form a gerund, add *-ing* to the base form of the verb.

We can use gerunds:

➤ as the subject or the object of a sentence.
Skiing can be dangerous.
I enjoy cooking.

➤ after prepositions.
I'm interested in collecting rocks.
He's bad at explaining things.

➤ after the verb *go* when we are talking about activities.
They go walking every weekend.
I often go sailing in the summer.

➤ after the verbs *feel, hear, listen to, notice, see* and *watch* to show that an action was in progress at a specific time.
I saw you opening the door.
I watched her coming down the street.

➤ after certain verbs and phrases.

admit (to)	imagine
avoid	involve
be used to	it's no good
can't help	it's no use
can't stand	it's (not) worth
consider	keep
delay	mention
deny	miss
dislike	postpone
(don't) mind	practice
enjoy	prevent from
feel like	risk
finish	spend time
have difficulty	suggest

He has difficulty controlling his temper.
It's not worth complaining about the food.

See "Gerund or Infinitive?" on page 122 for information on other verbs that can be followed by gerunds.

1 ▶ Complete the sentences with the gerund form of the words in the box.

help   ~~kill~~   learn   live   sail   say   speak   stay   tell

Ex.   *We can't prevent hunters from ....killing............ animals.*

1   Are you used to ....living.......... in this city now?

2   There's no point in ....Telling.......... lies. We already know the truth.

3   I dislike ....Sailing.........., but I love skiing.

4   Do you think it's worth ....Staying.... in tonight and watching TV?

5   Now that you've moved to Texas, I miss ....Speaking.. to you every day.

6   Why does he object to ....heping.......... us paint the garage?

7   Forgive me for ....Saying.......... this, but I think you're being unreasonable.

8   My cousin's interested in ....Learning.......... how to windsurf.

2 ▶ Find the mistakes and rewrite the sentences correctly.

Ex.   *What about to watch a video this evening?*
   What about watching a video this evening?...

1   He always goes for fishing on Sundays.

   ....

2   I often have difficulty to hearing what she's saying.

   ....

3   I'm thinking about start a company that upgrades computers.

   ....

4   The rock climb is an extremely dangerous sport.

   ....

5   When are we going to shopping?

   ....

6   I'm not used to have so much responsibility.

   ....

7   How can we prevent people to destroying our beautiful environment?

   ....

8   What's the use of learn English if you never use it?

   ....

9   I can't imagine the living without electricity.

   ....

10   Do you think he's interested apply for the job?

   ....

Infinitives with To

The infinitive is formed by adding *to* before the base form of a verb. It is sometimes called the full infinitive. We use the infinitive:

➤ to express purpose.
She went to the post office to send a package to her friend in San Diego.

➤ after certain verbs and phrases.

afford	choose	learn how	pretend
agree	decide	manage	promise
appear	expect	need	refuse
arrange	fail	offer	seem
ask	forget	plan	want
be allowed	hope	prepare	would like

They agreed to come to the meeting.
They forgot to lock the door.
They learned how to drive last summer.

➤ after the verbs *ask, decide, know, learn, remember, understand*, etc., when they are followed by a question word (*who, what*, etc.). However, we don't use the infinitive after *why*. We use subject + verb.
I didn't know what to say.
I understood how to operate the machine.
I don't know why she said that.

➤ after adjectives like *afraid, angry, anxious, ashamed, glad, happy, kind, nice, pleased, sad, sorry, stupid, surprised, upset, willing*, etc.
I'm ashamed to say I lost your book.
He's happy to be in this group.
Was she surprised to hear that she failed?

➤ after the words *too* and *enough*.
She's too afraid to tell the truth.
I haven't bought enough cakes to give one to each person.

➤ with *only* to talk about an unsatisfactory result.
I walked for two hours only to find I was in the wrong area.

The verbs *allow, invite* and *persuade* are followed by an object pronoun or noun before the infinitive.
His manager allowed him to leave early.

See "Gerund or Infinitive?" on page 122 for information on other verbs that can be followed by infinitives.

---

3 ▶ Complete the sentences with the infinitive form of the verbs in the box.

admit	find	go	hear	relax	say	see	wait	work

Ex. *They didn't have time* ....*to wait*............ *for us any longer.*

1 I was surprised .... your boss at the movies last night.
2 They don't know how .... they're sorry for what happened.
3 I'm willing .... late every evening this week if it helps you.
4 We ran to their house only .... that they had already left.
5 It was too cold .... swimming.
6 I was very pleased .... about your promotion.
7 He's ashamed .... it, but he's the one who broke the window.
8 They went on vacation ....

4 ▶ Complete the sentences with infinitives or gerunds.

Ex. *It's no use* ....*cooking*............ *chicken because she's a vegetarian. (cook)*

1 You were very kind .... me such a nice present. (bring)
2 My favorite hobby is .... (paint)
3 I can't get used to .... everyone speaking Spanish. (hear)
4 He went into town .... some shopping. (do)
5 Forgive me for .... you to lend me some money. (ask)
6 He was sorry .... the company after such a long time. (leave)
7 I can't decide who .... this book to. (give)
8 How about .... to some of our new CDs? (listen)

Infinitives without To

The infinitive without *to* is also called the base form of the verb. We use it after:

➤ modal verbs.
You must say exactly what you mean.
He should be more polite.
You can't park there.

➤ the verbs *feel, hear, listen to, notice, see* and *watch* to describe a completed action.
I heard Tom ask his boss if he could leave early.
I saw her take the bracelet.

➤ the phrases *had better* and *would rather*.
You had better study for the test.
He'd rather not shop for computers until they go on sale.

5 ▶ **Complete the sentences with the correct infinitive form.**

~~buy~~   go   help   install   not watch   refuse   tell   wear   work   write

Ex.   *I might .... buy .... a car next year.*

1   He doesn't have enough patience .... as a nurse or a teacher.
2   They agreed .... the computer for us.
3   I'd rather .... TV right now.
4   What can I .... to the costume party?
5   It was silly of him .... the offer.
6   I'd better .... home now.
7   I'm too upset .... you about it at the moment.
8   He watched me .... the reports and didn't offer .... at all.

6 ▶ **Choose the correct answer.**

Ex.   *I feel like .... for a walk.*
      a to go   *b go*   ⓒ *going*

1   He was seen .... a wallet into his pocket.
    a put   **b** to put   **c** putting
2   I want .... to a French university and study European languages.
    a go   **b** to go   **c** going
3   I can't get used to .... on icy roads.
    a drive   **b** to drive   **c** driving
4   He'd rather not .... full time, but he needs the money.
    a work   **b** to work   **c** working
5   I think you should .... some professional advice.
    a seek   **b** to seek   **c** seeking
6   He is very good at ....
    a cycle   **b** to cycle   **c** cycling
7   I bought my cousin a detective novel only .... that he'd already read it.
    a discover   **b** to discover   **c** discovering
8   What's the point of .... angry whenever I make a mistake?
    a get   **b** to get   **c** getting

7 ▶ **Complete the text with the correct form of the verb in parentheses.**

Last weekend my friend and I decided (Ex.) ....*to go*........ (go) on an adventure vacation. We considered

(1) .... (spend) a weekend in the mountains, but we aren't used to (2) .... (climb).

In the end we agreed (3) .... (go) (4) .... (camp) in a forest. Both of us wanted

(5) .... (learn) more about the wildlife in forests, so the trip seemed (6) .... (be) the

best way of (7) .... (do) this. When we got there, we expected (8) .... (find)

the tents all ready for us. We were surprised (9) .... (discover) that we had to put them up

ourselves. We felt like (10) .... (turn around) and (11) .... (go) back home, but

we didn't! After a short while we started enjoying ourselves. We kept (12) .... (discover) new

things about the forest. For example, we hadn't expected (13) .... (be able to) pick mushrooms and

cook them for breakfast. By the end of the weekend, we weren't looking forward to (14) .... (go) home

at all. We wanted (15) .... (stay) in the forest forever!

Gerund or Infinitive?

Some verbs can be followed by the gerund or infinitive with no change in meaning:

➤ begin, bother, continue, hate, like, love, start.
The orchestra began playing/to play at 8 o'clock.
Don't bother waiting/to wait for me.
He continued walking/to walk down the street.
I hate reading/to read boring books.
It started raining/to rain as soon as we left the house!

Other verbs can be followed by the gerund or the infinitive, but the meaning changes:

➤ forget, go on, regret, remember, stop, try.
He's forgotten meeting you before. (forget + gerund = not remember a past action)
I forgot to say where I was going. (forget + infinitive = forget, then fail to act)

They went on watching TV. (go on + gerund = continue doing something)
They went on to buy some shoes. (go on + infinitive = finish one thing and start another)

I regret telling him about my problem. (regret + gerund = have second thoughts about a past action)
I regret to say that you've failed your driving test. (regret + infinitive = feel bad about what is about to be said or done)

She remembers leaving water for the dog. (remember + gerund = recall doing something in the past)
I hope she remembers to leave water for the dog. (remember + infinitive = recall, then act)

The lesson was boring, so they stopped listening. (stop + gerund = finish, quit doing something)
They were talking quietly. When the lesson began, they stopped to listen. (stop + infinitive = finish one action in order to do another)

Try studying without the TV on. (try + gerund = experiment)
Try not to worry. (try + infinitive = make an attempt to do something)

8 ▶ **Complete the sentences with gerunds or infinitives.**

Ex. *He tried* ....*to speak*........... *to her on the phone, but he couldn't get through. (speak)*

1   Does she regret .... to college? (not go)
2   You should stop .... before you fall asleep at the wheel. (rest)
3   We regret .... you that another candidate has been offered the job. (tell)
4   Stop .... and talk to me calmly! (shout)
5   Don't look so surprised to see me. Have you forgotten .... me to the meeting? (invite)
6   Did he remember .... the cat this morning? (feed)
7   The speaker went on .... about her research even though the audience knew all about it. (talk)
8   I forgot .... her if she had had a good time. (ask)

9 ▶ **Find the extra word in each sentence and write it on the dotted line.**

Ex. *I regret to telling you what she said about you.* ......*to*......

1   We should have be kinder to her. ....
2   He has forgot to lock the door. ....
3   Why did you stop have going to karate classes? ....
4   Would you mind I telling me what to do? ....
5   When did you do arrange to go to New York? ....
6   I dislike it watching sports on TV. ....

10 ▶ **Check (✓) the correct sentence.**

Ex. *Are you thinking about going away for the weekend?* ___✓___
    Are you thinking about to go away for the weekend? ____

1   It's no use to study an hour before the exam! ____
    It's no use studying an hour before the exam! ____
2   He refuses helping her after their argument. ____
    He refuses to help her after their argument. ____
3   I promise to bring you back a souvenir from my trip to Brazil. ____
    I promise bring you back a souvenir from my trip to Brazil. ____
4   Jane would rather playing the guitar than the piano. ____
    Jane would rather play the guitar than the piano. ____
5   Our friends regret moving from their hometown. ____
    Our friends regret to move from their hometown. ____
6   He sometimes has great difficulty to explain what he means. ____
    He sometimes has great difficulty explaining what he means. ____

11 ▶ **Complete the sentences using your own words. Use gerunds and infinitives.**

Ex. *I enjoy* ...*traveling on my own.*...

1   I am looking forward to ....
2   I can't stand ....
3   Last year I began ....
4   I'm not allowed ....
5   I spend time ....
6   I want to know how ....

Pairwork

Work with a partner. Ask and answer questions using gerunds and infinitives. For example:

Student A: *What do you feel like doing this evening?*
Student B: *I feel like going to the movies.*

Student B: *What did you refuse to do yesterday?*
Student A: *I refused to cook dinner!*

Writing

Write an e-mail to your friend. Talk about what you've been doing and what's happened to you during the past week. Use sentences with gerunds and infinitives.

Wish / If Only

We use *wish/if only* to talk about a situation that isn't or wasn't as we want or wanted it to be. *If only* is used to give more emphasis, and it is not used in questions.

We use *wish/if only* + Simple Past/Past Continuous when we wish something was different in the present.
I wish I had more money.
If only he were feeling better.

We use *wish/if only* + Past Perfect/Past Perfect Continuous when we wish something had been different in the past.
I wish I hadn't said that.
If only he hadn't been driving so fast.

We use *wish/if only* + *would* + base form of verb:

➤ when we want something to change in the future.
  I wish you would be more careful.
  If only you would stop lying.

➤ to talk about something that someone does that annoys us. It is used for present situations.
  I wish you would stop arguing.
  If only they would make less noise.

Notes

In wishes about the present with the verb *to be*, we usually use *were* for all subjects.
I wish you were more patient.
If only she were less bossy.

1 ▸ **Complete the sentences with the Simple Past or Past Perfect.**

Ex. *If only we .... had arrived .... earlier. (arrive)*

1   I wish you .... my friend. (be)
2   If only they .... so rude to their neighbors last week. (not be)
3   I wish I .... more people at this party. (know)
4   He wishes he .... her to marry him. (ask)
5   Do you sometimes wish you .... a bigger house? (have)
6   If only you .... me sooner, I would have come. (tell)
7   My brother wishes the weather .... so cold! (not be)
8   I wish you .... so far away. (not live)

2 ▸ **Write sentences using the words in parentheses.**

Ex. *I don't have enough money. (more)*
     I wish ...I had more money...........................

1   He is living in a tiny apartment. (larger)
    He wishes ....
    ....

2   Our dog chewed everybody's shoes. (his toys)
    If only ....
    ....

3   I don't have the chance to travel very often. (more often)
    If only I ....
    ....

4   She was talking during the meeting. (listen)
    She wishes ....
    ....

5   He is rude to customers. (more polite)
    If only ....
    ....

6   She owns an old bicycle. (new sports car)
    She wishes ....
    ....

3 ▸ **Rewrite the sentences using the words given. Use between two and five words.**

Ex. *My friend talks very fast.* **would**
     I .... wish my friend would talk .... more slowly.

1   They drop litter in the streets. **only**
    If .... drop litter in the streets.

2   My son can't understand his math homework. **could**
    My son .... his math homework.

3   My computer was damaged in the flood. **been**
    If only my computer .... in the flood.

4   It would be nice if theater tickets weren't so expensive. **cheaper**
    If only .... than they are.

5   James is unemployed at the moment. **find**
    James wishes he .... a job.

6   It's been raining for days. **stop**
    I wish .... raining.

7   Meg regrets staying home last summer. **stayed**
    Meg wishes .... last summer.

8   He never helps me with the dishes. **would**
    I wish .... with the dishes.

Wish + Infinitive

We use *wish* + infinitive for something we want to do. It has the same meaning as *want*, but it is more formal. The subject of *wish* must be the same as the subject of the infinitive.
I wish to make a complaint.
The boss wishes to see you in her office immediately.

Notes

Wish + somebody + something is sometimes used in good wishes/greetings.
We wish you a pleasant stay at our hotel.
I wish you the best of luck in the future.

Hope

We use *hope* + (*that*) + clause in the past, the present and the future to express a desire about something likely or possible.
I hope (that) you don't mind waiting.
I hope (that) he wasn't hurt.
I hope (that) they'll be able to meet us.

We use *hope* + infinitive for intentions. Like *wish* + infinitive, the subject of *hope* must be the same as the subject of the infinitive.
I hope to buy a new laptop this weekend.
She hopes to get a job very soon.

---

4 ▷ **Complete the sentences with the correct Simple Present form of hope or wish.**

Ex.   *Kevin ......hopes...... he will be chosen for the football team.*

1   David .... she likes her present.

2   We .... he didn't live so far away.

3   I .... you had a good time at the theater.

4   They .... she didn't get lost in the forest.

5   Lucy .... her family lived closer to her.

6   Many people .... they were rich.

---

5 ▷ **Complete the sentences with the infinitive form of the verbs in the box.**

| be | buy | complain | congratulate | express | find | have | know | move |

Ex.   *I hope ......to move...... to California next year.*

1   I wish .... about the poor service at this hotel.

2   I hope .... a famous artist one day.

3   I wish .... my warmest congratulations on your promotion.

4   I hope .... a better job than this one very soon!

5   I wish .... you on the success of your new novel.

6   I hope .... a house within the next year or two.

7   I wish .... what you're doing here.

8   I hope .... some better news for you before too long.

6 ▶ **Complete the sentences in your own words.**

Ex.   *I hope I* ......*will find a well-paid job when I graduate college.*......

1   I hope I ....

2   I hope my best friend ....

3   I wish ....

4   I wish you ....

5   I hope my family ....

6   I wish to ....

7   I hope our neighbors ....

8   I hope my children ....

Would Rather & Prefer

We use *would rather* to express preference.

When we want to express someone's preference about themselves, we use the following structures:

➤ subject + *would rather* + base form of verb (present/future)
He'd rather play football later.

➤ subject + *would rather* + *have* + past participle (past)
They'd rather have gone to the Chinese restaurant.

When we want to express someone's preference about another person's actions, we use the following structures:

➤ subject 1 + *would rather* + subject 2 + Simple Past/Past Continuous (present/future)
(Note: When we use the Simple Past of *be* or the Past Continuous in this structure, we usually use *were* for all subjects.)
Our parents would rather we took the train.
He's in Mexico now, but I'd rather he were here with us. I miss him.
They'd rather she were going with them.

➤ subject 1 + *would rather* + subject 2 + Past Perfect (past)
His parents would rather he had finished college.

We can also use the structures above with *than* to express a preference for one thing or action over another thing or action:
I'd rather listen to rock than jazz. (I like listening to rock more than I like listening to jazz)
He'd rather read a book than watch a movie. (He prefers reading a book to watching jazz.)
Her parents would rather she went to Harvard than Yale. (They want her to go to Harvard, not Yale.)

We also use *prefer* for preferences.

➤ *prefer* + noun/gerund + *to* + noun/gerund (general preference)
They prefer tennis to basketball.
He prefers driving to walking.
I prefer going to the movies to watching DVDs at home.

➤ *prefer* + infinitive + *rather than* + base form of verb (general preference)
John prefers to eat at home rather than go to a restaurant.
I prefer to travel by plane rather than go by train.

➤ *would prefer* + infinitive + *rather than* + base form of verb (specific preference)
Freda would prefer to visit Paris rather than visit Rome this summer. (She usually goes to Rome every summer.)
I would prefer to do this now rather than do it tomorrow.

7 ► **Write sentences.**

Ex. *own a dog / a cat*
I'd prefer ...*to own a dog rather than a cat.*..

1 stay in a hotel / camp in a tent

We'd rather ....

2 go to bed now / stay up late

I'd prefer ....

3 coffee / tea

I prefer ....

4 travel by plane / by boat

He prefers ....

5 listen to music / study archaeology

He'd rather ....

6 eat meat / fish

She'd rather ....

8 ► **Choose the correct answer.**

Ex. *I'd rather .... to town this afternoon than stay here and read my book.*

   a to go   *b going*   Ⓒ *go*

1 They'd rather .... pasta than rice yesterday evening.

   a eat   **b** be eating   **c** have eaten

2 Would you rather .... your money on clothes than CDs?

   a spend   **b** have spend   **c** to spend

3 They would rather I .... dinner more often.

   a cook   **b** cooked   **c** was cooking

4 Do you prefer .... windsurf rather than waterski?

   a to   **b** can   **c** would

5 He said he'd prefer .... out for dinner tonight.

   a to go   **b** have gone   **c** go

6 I'd rather .... last summer in Boston than in New York.

   a have spent   **b** spend   **c** be spending

7 We'd rather they .... their dog to our house last night.

   a haven't brought   **b** to bring   **c** hadn't brought

8 She prefers wearing jeans .... skirts.

   a for   **b** than   **c** to

9 ▶ Rewrite the sentences using the words given. Use between two and five words.

Ex. *I don't really want to do the dishes.* **rather**

I .... *would rather not do* .... the dishes.

1 I didn't go to the concert last night, but I wanted to. **would**

I .... to the concert last night.

2 I prefer reading a book to watching a boring program on TV. **than**

I would .... watch a boring program on TV.

3 I would prefer her to ask me herself. **asked**

I .... me herself.

4 I wish you hadn't spent so much on my birthday present. **less**

I would .... on my birthday present.

5 I'm at home this evening and I don't want to be. **out**

I .... with my friends this evening.

6 She is sorry now that she agreed to go on vacation with them next month. **going**

She would .... on vacation with them next month.

7 I'd rather not get up right now. **stay**

I .... in bed right now.

8 I don't like it when you arrive late. **rather**

I'd .... arrive late.

10 ▶ Find the mistakes and rewrite the sentences correctly.

Ex. *I'd rather they didn't came here again.*

I'd rather they didn't come here again.

1 I'd rather it hasn't rained every day when we were in San Francisco last month.

....

2 She'd rather eat at the Chinese restaurant to the Indian restaurant.

....

3 I would rather you didn't started smoking again.

....

4 They would rather I have taken a job closer to home.

....

5 We'd prefer to watching a comedy rather than a thriller.

....

6 I'd rather not have drink any more coffee today.

....

Pairwork

Work with a partner. Read the following situation and then talk about it using the phrases you have learned in this unit.

Douglas had an argument with his boss and now they aren't speaking. He wanted to buy himself a new laptop, so he borrowed some money from his boss. He didn't return the money on time. Then his boss took him to court. Douglas was so angry that he drove his car too fast and had an accident in which he broke his leg. He is now in the hospital.

For example:

Douglas wishes he hadn't argued with his boss. He would rather he and his boss were speaking to each other again. If only they hadn't had an argument. He'd prefer ...

Writing

Imagine you have been asked to write a report for a magazine. The title of your report is *I Wish ... .* Remember to talk about the past, the present and the future.

....
....
....
....
....
....
....
....
....
....
....
....
....
....
....
....

Review 4 (Units 13-16)

1 ▷ Choose the correct answer.

Ex. *I couldn't find any rices /(pasta) in the cupboard, so I went out and bought some.*

1 We'd like two *lemonades / lemonade*, please.

2 I don't know how he'll cope now that he is a *widow / widower*.

3 We need to repair *some / any* of the furniture we have been given for our new house.

4 Sharpening the kitchen *knifes / knives* is not a job I enjoy.

5 Make sure you take some *cans / bags* of soup with you when you go camping.

6 At 70 years old, my grandfather still had a full head of *hairs / hair*.

7 He has worn *glass / glasses* since he was two years old.

8 There's no *rooms / room* in that closet for anything else.

2 ▷ Complete with a, an, the or –.

Ex. *When I saw ....the.... manager of ....the.... hotel, I complained to him about ....the.... food.*

1 Who was .... person I saw you with in .... park yesterday?

2 Let's have .... breakfast together in .... morning.

3 We are planning .... vacation in Italy. We'll fly to .... Rome, and then take .... tour of the city by .... bus.

4 For people who don't have .... ability to live on their own, ... life can't be easy.

5 Do you remember the name of .... place we visited when we went to .... New York last month?

6 I saw .... amazing thing when I went on .... sightseeing tour of Mexico City.

7 Do you feel like going to one of .... Chinese restaurants in town this evening? If not, we could order .... meal

   from .... Indian restaurant on the corner and watch .... TV at home.

8 The speaker told us about some of .... things that we can do to save .... environment.

3 ▷ Choose the correct answer.

Ex. *How .... time do we have before we board the plane?*
   a *many*   **b** *lot*   **c** *much*

1 I couldn't decide which CD to buy, so I didn't buy ....
   a both   **b** neither   **c** either
2 The .... class was punished because of their poor behavior.
   a all   **b** whole   **c** every
3 There are .... choices for dessert. What do you feel like?
   a a little   **b** a lot   **c** a few
4 I can stay for .... while, but then I'll have to leave as I have a doctor's appointment.
   a a little   **b** a lot   **c** a few
5 There don't seem to be .... opportunities for promotion in your company.
   a much   **b** a lot   **c** many
6 .... my cousin nor my brother ever wears jeans anymore.
   a Both   **b** Either   **c** Neither
7 .... the people I know are looking forward to the next Olympics.
   a Whole   **b** All   **c** Every
8 .... of my friends ever goes fishing.
   a All   **b** Both   **c** None

4 ▸ Rewrite the sentences using the words given. Use between two and five words.

Ex. *It's possible that this is the answer to all our problems.* **could**
    This ....could be the answer.................. to all our problems.

1   Do you think it's possible that Jane has been promoted? **could**
    Do you think .... promoted?

2   Perhaps he has been delayed because he's lost. **may**
    He .... he's lost.

3   It's possible for her to be here before nine. **can**
    She .... before nine.

4   Should we buy a book for Shirley? **could**
    We .... for Shirley.

5   Is it possible for you to hold the ladder for me while I climb up? **can**
    .... for me while I climb up?

6   Is it possible they will agree to our plans? **may**
    Do you think .... our plans?

7   He was lucky he didn't break his leg when he jumped off the stone wall. **could**
    He .... when he jumped off the stone wall.

8   It is possible that our friends were delayed by the accident on the highway. **may**
    Our friends .... by the accident on the highway.

5 ▸ Choose the correct answer.

Ex. *You* can't*/ couldn't be cold; it's like a sauna in here!*

1   That *can / must* be the reason why she hasn't called us.

2   You *couldn't / can* have seen the DVD of that movie because it hasn't been released yet.

3   He *can't / must* have understood a word. He doesn't speak any German.

4   She *can't / must* have passed her driving test. I see her driving all over town now.

5   That *can't / mustn't* be your jacket. It's at least two sizes too small for you.

6   He *must / may not* have meant to be so rude. He's always so polite.

7   They aren't answering the phone, but it *must / might* be their lunch hour.

8   It *might / couldn't* have been my cousin you saw. He's on vacation in Germany.

6 ▸ Complete the sentences with must, might or can't.

Ex. *You ......must...... be a very good cook if you've made all this wonderful food yourself!*

1   I think I .... be transferred to the Seattle office.

2   I'm not sure where she is. She .... have gone shopping for some new clothes.

3   Your mom .... have been very young when she had you if you're 30 now and she's only 48.

4   He .... come to the meeting. He said he'd let us know.

5   It .... have been my sister you spoke to on the phone because she's on a business trip this week.

6   He .... have heard the good news about her promotion. He just called to congratulate her.

7   You .... become famous if you start doing some singing at local concerts.

8   I .... believe you're a doctor now! You seem too young!

7 ▶ **Choose the correct answer.**

Ex. *I don't understand why you won't consider .... to the museum with me.*
   a *to come*   **b** *comes*   **ⓒ** *coming*

1 How can we prevent him from .... up his job and leaving the country?
   a giving   **b** to give   **c** give

2 I'm afraid .... you what I've done.
   a tell   **b** to tell   **c** telling

3 Don't get upset. You can easily .... another job.
   a find   **b** to find   **c** finding

4 It was extremely kind of you .... this beautiful plant for me.
   a bringing   **b** bring   **c** to bring

5 I don't know which movie .... to.
   a go   **b** going   **c** to go

6 Do you have time .... shopping with me on Saturday?
   a to go   **b** going   **c** go

7 I'm ashamed of .... the way I did.
   a to behave   **b** behave   **c** behaving

8 We listened to the birds .... in the tree.
   a to sing   **b** singing   **c** to be singing

8 ▶ **Complete with gerunds or infinitives.**

Ex. *He seems ....to be................ pleased with his new bike. (be)*

1 I don't expect .... at your house much before midnight. (arrive)

2 They suggest .... to Prague for their next holiday. (go)

3 He tried .... the report today, but he ran out of time. (finish)

4 Can you ever .... me for being so rude? (forgive)

5 Can you stop .... that for a minute and listen to me? (do)

6 You have no excuse for .... to the meeting. (not come)

7 I've asked .... a day off at the end of the week so I can see you. (take)

8 I'd rather not .... this evening; let's eat out instead. (cook)

9 ▶ **Check (✓) the correct sentence.**

Ex. *I'm too lazy writing letters every day. _____*
   I'm too lazy to write letters every day. __✓__

1 The food was too spicy for me to eat. _____
   The food was too spicy for me too eat. _____

2 I love to be lie on a sandy beach and read a good book. _____
   I love to lie on a sandy beach and read a good book. _____

3 You might want to see the play, but I'm not taking you! _____
   You might want to seeing the play, but I'm not taking you! _____

4 Production at the car plant appears to been falling lately. _____
   Production at the car plant appears to have fallen lately. _____

5 Do you feel like to get involved in one of the local environmental groups? _____
   Do you feel like getting involved in one of the local environmental groups? _____

6 I really miss talking to you on the phone every day. _____
   I really miss to talk to you on the phone every day. _____

7 I'd better to get back to work now. _____
   I'd better get back to work now. _____

8 He's decided to leave home and get his own apartment in the city. _____
   He's decided to leave home and getting his own apartment in the city. _____

10 ▶ Rewrite the sentences using the words given. Use between two and five words.

Ex.   *I would like to have a new car.* **had**
      I ....wish I had........... a new car.

1   If it was sunny, we could go out and walk for an hour. **were**
    I .... so we could go out and walk for an hour.
2   I feel bad that Bill didn't call me today. **had**
    I .... me today.
3   He keeps on hitting his brother and I want him to stop doing it. **would**
    If only .... his brother.
4   I think it would be a good idea if you looked for somewhere else to live. **wish**
    I .... for somewhere else to live.
5   I'd like it if we could go out together every weekend. **could**
    I .... together every weekend.
6   I'm not an actor but I'd like to be one. **were**
    I .... an actor.

11 ▶ Choose the correct answer.

Ex.   *I would* prefer / (rather) *see a play than a movie this weekend.*

1   Apparently, he *prefers / would rather* snowboarding to skiing these days.
2   She hopes *being / to be* one of the top executives in the company within five years.
3   I'd rather you *hadn't / haven't* told anyone about how I copied the information off the Internet.
4   We would *rather / prefer* wear jeans to work, but our boss makes us wear more formal business clothes.
5   *Had / Would* you prefer to go horseback riding or roller skating?
6   I *hope / wish* you success in your new career as a driving instructor.
7   I'd rather you *did / do* the typing because I don't type very fast.
8   He would *rather not / prefer not* have been a witness in the court case.

12 ▶ Find the mistakes and rewrite the sentences correctly.

Ex.   *We hope going to the same college.*
      We hope to go to the same college. ....

1   He would rather to not buy her a diamond engagement ring, but she insists on it.
    ....

2   Would you prefer to coming with us this evening or stay at home?
    ....

3   The manager would prefer he will speak to you in private.
    ....

4   If only they wish would show more good movies on TV.
    ....

5   I wish I know more people in my neighborhood.
    ....

6   We walked for five miles yesterday, and now I wish we didn't!
    ....

135

Advice – Should / Ought To

She shouldn't stay up so late.
Should I make hotel reservations today?
You should be trying harder at work.

He ought to take his camera on vacation with him.
He ought to be getting ready for work, but he's
still in bed.

We use *should(n't)* and *ought to* + the base form of a verb or *be* + *-ing* to give advice.
You should make vacation plans well in advance. You shouldn't wait till the last minute.
We ought to look for a cheaper apartment.
You ought to be studying now. You shouldn't be watching TV.

We use *should* to ask for advice.
Should I buy these shoes?
Should we offer to help?

Notes

Ought to is not used in questions.
The form *ought not to* is rarely used in American English.

---

1 ▶ **Complete the sentences with should or shouldn't and the words in parentheses.**

Ex.   He ....*should wash*............. his shirt now. *(wash)*

1   I .... fried foods. (give up)

2   You .... hard for the race. (train)

3   .... my computer serviced? (I / have)

4   Our son .... so much time playing computer games. (spend)

5   The doctor said I .... more rest. (get)

6   .... him to paint our house? (we / ask)

7   You .... your hairstyle if you want to look more stylish. (change)

8   He .... to work today. He isn't feeling well. (go)

9   The boss .... you a raise. You're a very valuable employee. (give)

10   You .... every weekend. You need some time to relax. (work)

2 ▸ Complete the sentences with ought to and a word or phrase from the box.

apologize   ask   be   be doing   be studying   ~~buy~~   catch   exercise   go

Ex.   *His car keeps breaking down. He* ....*ought to buy*............ *a new one.*

1   If you want to lose weight, you .... more.

2   The government .... more to make people conserve energy.

3   If you want to make the boss happy, you .... on time every day.

4   The children are always tired in the morning. They .... to bed earlier.

5   She's still mad at you for what you did. You .... to her.

6   You look like you need a vacation. You .... for some time off.

7   His exams are next week. He .... every night.

8   You're always late for work. You .... an earlier train.

3 ▸ Write advice using should or ought to and your own words.

Ex.   *My brother eats several bars of chocolate a day.*

      He should/ought to stop eating so much chocolate! ....

1   Their boss makes them do far too much work.

     ....

2   People leave their trash on the beach.

     ....

3   I've never liked the color of my bedroom walls.

     ....

4   His room is a mess.

     ....

5   My brother doesn't go out very much.

     ....

6   My best friend isn't speaking to me at the moment.

     ....

7   I want to buy a car.

     ....

8   I don't know how to use a computer very well.

     ....

Criticism – Should / Ought To

Affirmative
I should/ought to have listened
you should/ought to have listened
he should/ought to have listened
she should/ought to have listened
it should/ought to have listened
we should/ought to have listened
you should/ought to have listened
they should/ought to have listened

Negative
I shouldn't have listened
you shouldn't have listened
he shouldn't have listened
she shouldn't have listened
it shouldn't have listened
we shouldn't have listened
you shouldn't have listened
they shouldn't have listened

We use *should/ought to* + *have* + base form of the verb to talk about something that would have been the right thing to do in the past, but that wasn't done.
You should have washed my car after you borrowed it.
I ought to have offered to stay and help clean up.

We use the negative form *shouldn't* + *have* + base form of the verb to talk about something that was done in the past, but that shouldn't have been done.
You shouldn't have left your keys inside the car.
He shouldn't have yelled at her during the meeting.

4 Complete the sentences with the past participles of the verbs from the box.

arrive   drive   follow   help   miss   speak   take   use   wash

Ex. *You should have ....arrived......... at the airport on time.*

1 He should have .... the advice the doctor gave him.

2 You shouldn't have .... the meeting.

3 She ought to have .... her mother with the dishes.

4 Those children shouldn't have .... to their parents so rudely.

5 I should have .... the kitchen floor this morning.

6 He shouldn't have .... when he was so tired.

7 You shouldn't have .... bleach to get the stain out of your blue T-shirt.

8 They ought to have .... a taxi. It was too far to walk.

5 Find the extra word in each sentence and write it on the dotted line.

Ex. *You should have been taken my advice ages ago. ....been.........*

1 I ought to not lose some weight. ....

2 You shouldn't have eat so much at lunch. ....

3 He should to be more careful when he is driving on narrow country roads. ....

4 Do you think we ought to be tell the boss what happened? ....

5 They shouldn't have not ridden their bicycles without helmets. ....

6 Should I be take up a new hobby? ....

7 You ought to have been studied business in college. ....

8 She should have gone taken the day off on her birthday. ....

Offers – I'll / Shall / Can / Could

'll go to the supermarket for you.
Shall I help you make the beds?
Can we do anything for the wedding?
Could I go to the store for you?

We use *I'll* in affirmative sentences to offer help.
I'll find the phone for you.

We use *shall*, *can* and *could* with *I* and *we* in the question form to offer help.
Shall I make some coffee?
Can we clean the living room for you?
Could I help you with that?

6 ▶ **Write offers using I'll.**

Ex. *The dishes need washing.*
     I'll wash the dishes.

1   The living room is dusty.

     ....

2   The windows need washing.

     ....

3   I haven't gone shopping yet.

     ....

4   This shirt needs ironing.

     ....

5   Lunch needs to be made.

     ....

7 ▶ **Write offers using shall, can or could and the words in parentheses.**

Ex. *Your brother's bike is broken. (fix)*
     Shall I fix it?

1   These shoes are dirty. (clean)

     ....

2   There is no fruit left. (buy)

     ....

3   Your cousin has finished using the computer. (turn off)

     ....

4   This letter needs to be mailed. (mail)

     ....

5   The sheets on the beds haven't been changed for a week. (change)

     ....

Suggestions – Shall / Can / Could

We use *shall*, *can* and *could* to make suggestions.

Shall we go to the movies tonight?
I can cook dinner for us later.
We could go to the Italian restaurant.

8 ▶ **Choose the correct answer.**

Dear Aunt Anna,

I'm writing to say I'm really looking forward to coming to stay with you next week. (Ex.) *I'll* / I should do lots of things to help you while I'm there. I (1) *can / would* make the beds every morning for you. And (2) *ought / shall* I clean the bathroom, too? I'd like to bring some food with me. I (3) *shouldn't / can* bake you a cake or buy you some nice pies from the bakery here. I (4) *could / ought* also do the ironing for you. I'm really good at that! And one more thing, Aunt Anna. I (5) *shouldn't / could* take all your old newspapers and bottles to the recycling center for you. (6) You *shall / shouldn't* be carrying all those heavy things yourself. I know the doctor has told you that you (7) *could / ought to* rest more. You (8) *can / should* do as you're told!

See you soon.

Love,
Sophie

9 ▸ **Write suggestions using the words in parentheses.**

Ex. *I'd like to see that new action movie. (shall / go / tonight)*
     Shall we go tonight? ....

1   I'm feeling hungry and I can't be bothered to cook. (could / make / lunch)
    ....

2   I don't want to go to town on my own. (shall / go / together)
    ....

3   I'm sad because I don't have anything nice to wear. (can / lend / suit)
    ....

4   I'd like to be better at tennis. (could / take lessons / sports center)
    ....

5   I'm interested in seeing the new exhibit at the art gallery. (shall / go / on Saturday)
    ....

6   I'd like to see you again. (can / go out / dinner)
    ....

7   I don't have time to take the children to the park. (could / take / for you)
    ....

8   We haven't been horseback riding in a while. (shall / go / on Sunday)
    ....

10 ▸ **Find the mistakes and rewrite the sentences correctly.**

Ex. *I think you shall cook more often.*
     I think you should cook more often. ....

1   Ought I help you to prepare the house for their visit?
    ....

2   I know! Will we go and see a play at the new theater tomorrow?
    ....

3   I really think you should to wait a few months before you ask for a promotion.
    ....

4   The doctor said I shall exercise more and lose some weight.
    ....

5   You should not threw all my old clothes away yesterday.
    ....

6   I know I shall visit her, but I'm just too busy this week.
    ....

7   My dentist says I will brush my teeth after every meal.
    ....

8   Could we took a break now?
    ....

11 Rewrite the sentences using the words given. Use between two and five words.

Ex. *I advise you to study art history.* **should**
   You ....should study.......... art history.

1 I want to make some sandwiches for the picnic. **shall**
   .... sandwiches for the picnic?

2 It would be a good idea for you to buy some new boots. **ought**
   You .... new boots.

3 I'd like us to go out for dinner tonight. **could**
   .... for dinner tonight.

4 It was wrong of him to have ignored his accountant. **not**
   He .... his accountant.

5 You should take some extra clothes with you. **to**
   You .... some extra clothes with you.

6 It wasn't a good thing that you drove so fast to get here. **not**
   You .... so fast to get here.

7 It would be a good idea for us go on a diet together. **we**
   .... a diet together?

Thinkaboutit

Use **have** + past participle after **should(n't)** and **ought to** to talk about the past.

Pairwork

Work with a partner. Read the situations below and discuss what advice you could give each person.

➤ Miss Martin is sixty years old. She lives on her own in the country and she is very lonely. She is healthy and she can drive. She likes cooking and reading. She doesn't know many people in her area, but she has a computer and she enjoys writing e-mails.

➤ Bradley Wilson is twenty-one years old. He likes motorcycles and is big fan of car racing, but he doesn't have a vehicle of his own. He is unemployed, but would like to get a job so he can earn some money to buy a motorcycle. He would like to get to know other people interested in cars and motorcycles.

Writing

You have been asked by the mayor of your town or city to write a report saying what is wrong with the area you live in and making some suggestions as to what could be done to improve it. Write a report using the modals you have learned in this unit.

....
....
....
....
....
....
....
....
....
....
....
....

Causative

Verb Form	Example
Simple Present	*I have my hair cut every month.*
Present Continuous	*I am having my hair cut now.*
Simple Past	*I had my hair cut last month.*
Past Continuous	*I was having my hair cut yesterday morning.*
Present Perfect	*I have had my hair cut.*
Present Perfect Continuous	*I have been having my hair cut.*
Past Perfect	*I had already had my hair cut.*
Past Perfect Continuous	*I had been having my hair cut.*
Future with *Will*	*I will have my hair cut.*
Future Continuous	*I will be having my hair cut.*
Future Perfect	*I will have had my hair cut by then.*
be going to	*I'm going to have my hair cut.*
Modals (present)	*I must have my hair cut.*
Modals (past)	*I should have had my hair cut.*

The causative is formed as follows:

have (in appropriate form) + object + past participle (of the main verb)
I have my hair dyed once a month.
She will have her wedding dress made out of silk.
I had had my teeth straightened before I was sixteen.

The object of the sentence must always come before the past participle.

We use the causative:

➤ to talk about an action done for us by another person or thing.
   My sister has had some shoes made. (She didn't make them; someone made them for her.)
   I am going to have my kitchen redesigned. (I'm not going to do it; someone else is.)

➤ to talk about something unpleasant that happened to us that we didn't want to happen.
   She had her bag stolen on the bus. (She didn't want anybody to steal it.)
   We had our car stolen. (We didn't want someone to steal it.)

Notes

In everyday speech we can use *get* instead of *have*.
We're getting our house painted tomorrow.

When we talk about unpleasant things, we don't use *get*.
I had my bike stolen while I was in town.

---

1 ▶ **Write C next to the sentences that are causative.**

Ex. *I am having my bike repaired tomorrow.* .....*C*.....

He is cutting the grass now. ....

1   I'm having a nice time on the beach. ....

2   The patient is having his temperature taken. ....

3   I have had a lot of food to eat today. ....

4   They had a meal prepared by Anthony the chef. ....

5   Our friend has had an operation. ....

6   The man had his foot examined. ....

7   I had my teeth checked by the dentist. ....

8   The dentist got a new chair. ....

---

2 ▶ **Write sentences with the causative. Use the Present Continuous.**

Ex. *The car needs servicing.*

I'm having it serviced tomorrow.
....

1   The washing machine needs repairing.
....

2   Your teeth need examining.
....

3   The kitchen needs painting.
....

4   My jeans need shortening.
....

5   The grass needs cutting.
....

---

3 ▶ **Complete the sentences with the causative. Use the Simple Past.**

Ex. *Henry* ....*had his car damaged*.............. *last night. (his car / damage)*

1   My brother .... by his friend's father. (bike / repair)

2   I .... by someone at the supermarket. (my bag / take)

3   We .... by some burglars. (our house / break into)

4   I .... by a soccer ball. (my nose / break)

5   My doctor .... by someone at the airport. (her passport / steal)

6   I .... by the tailor. (my suit / take in)

---

4 ▶ **Complete the sentences with the causative. Use the Present Perfect or the Past Perfect.**

Ex. *They* ....*had had all the work done*.............. *by the middle of the day. (all the work / do)*

1   She .... since I last saw her. (her hair / cut)

2   I .... before I moved in. (my new apartment / paint)

3   My brother .... , but he hasn't picked it up from the garage yet. (car / repair)

4   We .... , so now I can do the laundry! (our washing machine / repair)

5   The writer .... before he began his last book. (computer / upgrade)

6   I .... this year. (my portrait / paint)

5 ▶ Write sentences in the causative. Use the words and verb forms in parentheses.

Ex.　We .... *will have had our fence fixed* .... by next week. (our fence / fix)
　　　(Future Perfect)

1　The bride .... by a French designer. (her dress / make)
　　(Future with Will)

2　I .... by the end of the month. (house / paint)
　　(Future Perfect)

3　They .... as soon as possible. (their carpets / clean)
　　(Future with Will)

4　They .... later this evening. (a pizza / deliver)
　　(Future Continuous)

5　She .... by a mail-order company. (some clothes / send)
　　(Future Continuous)

---

6 ▶ Complete the questions and write answers.

Ex.　(She / her knee / operate) ✗
　　　Is she having her knee operated .... on next week?
　　　No, she isn't. ....

1　(he / his coat / dry-clean) ✓
　　.. last week?
　　..

2　(he / his speech / write) ✗
　　.. by his wife?
　　..

3　(they / their house / paint) ✓
　　.. last July?
　　..

4　(you / your photos / develop) ✓
　　.. before
　　I see you next?
　　..

5　(she / her rose garden / plant) ✓
　　.. recently?
　　..

6　(he / his computer / upgrade) ✗
　　.. soon?
　　..

---

7 ▶ Find the extra word in each sentence.

Ex.　My brother had had it our TV repaired before I
　　　got home yesterday. ....*it*........

1　They did had the flower arrangements done
　　by a professional. ....

2　We are going to be have our heating system
　　replaced soon. ....

3　I'm having my eyes had tested tomorrow
　　morning. ....

4　I had having a package delivered by a courier
　　yesterday. ....

5　He sometimes has his reports are written by
　　his assistant. ....

6　She was had the cut stitched by the doctor in
　　the emergency room. ....

7　We have our letters are delivered by a mail
　　carrier who rides a motorcycle. ....

8　She has to had her passport and all her credit
　　cards stolen. ....

8 ▶ **Rewrite the sentences using the words given. Use between two and five words.**

Ex.   *The tailor shortened Jack's new suit.* **had**
      Jack ....*had his new suit shortened*............. *by the tailor.*

1   A doctor examined my knee last night. **by**
     I .... a doctor last night.

2   The boss has arranged for our office to be repainted next week. **having**
     The boss .... next week.

3   A mechanic will have repaired his car by tomorrow afternoon. **been**
     His car .... tomorrow afternoon.

4   The electrician is fixing our boiler tomorrow. **fixed**
     We .... tomorrow.

5   A professional photographer is taking our photo next weekend. **are**
     We .... by a professional photographer next weekend.

6   A gardener is going to plant rosebushes in their yard next month. **having**
     They .... in their yard next month.

Pairwork

Work with a partner. Take turns. Ask and answer questions about some of the things you have had done recently. For example:

Have you had your teeth checked recently?
Have you had a meal cooked for you recently?

Writing

Imagine you are extremely rich and famous. Write an e-mail to an old friend telling him/her about all the things that you now have done for you. Use your imagination!

145

Indirect Questions

We use indirect questions to ask for information politely.
They are introduced by a number of phrases.

Could you let me know ...?
Can you tell me ...?
Do you know ...?
Have you any idea ...?
I would like to know ... .
I wonder if you know ... .
I would like to ask you ... .
I don't suppose you know ... .

When a direct question becomes an indirect question, the word order changes from question form to statement form.

When the question begins with a question word (*who, what, where, which*, etc.), we form the indirect question with the same question word.
Where is the bank. → *Do you know where the bank is?*

When there isn't a question word in the direct question, we use *if* or *whether*.
Did the children enjoy the museum? → *Do you know if/whether the children enjoyed the museum?*

1 ▶ **Complete the indirect questions.**

Ex. *How much do snowboarding lessons cost?*
Could you tell me ..*how much snowboarding lessons cost?* ....

1 When did the car factory start production?
Do you know ....

2 Who starred in the movie *Titanic*?
I wonder if you know ....

3 Are there any eating facilities at the museum?
Do you know ....

4 What is the date of their wedding anniversary?
I don't suppose you know ....

5 Who did they award the Nobel Peace Prize to last year?
Have you any idea ....

6 Do any of those buses go to Detroit?
Can you tell me ....

7 Where are all the cables for this computer?
I would like to know ....

8 Why didn't the bank manager agree to lend you the money?
Do you know ....

Subject / Object Questions

Subject Questions
When the question word asks about the subject of a sentence, the word order doesn't change.
Susan called your cousin last night. ➜ *Who called your cousin last night?*
These books are mine. ➜ *Which books are yours?*

Object Questions
When the question word asks about the object of a sentence, the word order changes to the question form.
She wants to buy an apartment. ➜ *What does she want to buy?*
He made that table. ➜ *Which table did he make?*

Notes

When the verb is followed by a preposition in an object question, the preposition is also used in the question.
She listened to the opera. ➜ *What did she listen to?*

2 ▶ **Complete the questions with who, what, where or which.**

Ex. ......*Who*...... *does he play tennis with?*

1 .... of those CDs would you like me to buy you?
2 .... is taking the guests on a tour of Hollywood?
3 .... are you going to Yellowstone National Park with?
4 .... did the boss ask you to do before you left work?
5 .... did you get that beautiful antique necklace?
6 .... are you going to give it to?
7 .... did you clean the oven with?
8 .... are they staying with when they are in New York?
9 .... did she say to the manager when she made her complaint?
10 .... pair of boots did you decide to buy?

3 ▶ **Write questions.**

Ex. *Who* ..*made her wedding dress?*...............................
Mrs. Jenkins made her wedding dress.

1 Whose ....
   This is Mike's family.

2 What ....
   I sent a big box of chocolates.

3 Which ....
   The blue car is Jane's.

4 Who ....
   He bought those flowers for his wife.

5 Which ....
   The first apartment was the biggest.

6 Why ....
   Kate left her job because she's moving to Mexico.

7 Who ....
   Mr. Hunter is the director.

8 Where ....
   She's gone to the drugstore.

Tag Questions

Tag questions are formed using the auxiliary verb that goes with the verb form in the main clause and a subject pronoun that relates to the subject in the main clause.
Tom travels a lot, doesn't he?
The children made a mess, didn't they?
She's stayed here before, hasn't she?
You've met my brother, haven't you?

When the main clause is affirmative, we use a negative tag question.
You will wait for me, won't you?
She's unhappy, isn't she?

When the main clause is negative, we use an affirmative tag question.
She wasn't very polite, was she?
You aren't really hungry, are you?

Some tag questions are made in a different way.
I am ..., aren't I?
Let's ..., shall we?
[Imperative form] ..., will you/won't you?
This/That is ..., isn't it?
These/Those are ..., aren't they?

When the subject of the sentence is *everybody, nobody, someone,* etc., we use *they* in the tag question.
Everybody has joined the demonstration, haven't they?
Nobody wants to do this job, do they?

We use tag questions:

➤ when we want to confirm something we believe.
   That man is very tall, isn't he?

➤ when we are sure of what we are saying.
   He failed the test, didn't he?
   (I saw the list of results.)

Notes

The meaning of tag questions depends on voice intonation. When we are sure about something, the tone of our voice falls during the tag question. When we aren't sure about what we're saying, the tone of our voice rises during the tag question.
Sure: *She's finished that book, hasn't she?* ↘
Unsure: *He hasn't missed the bus again, has he?* ↗

4 ▶ Complete each sentence with a tag question from the box.

| are they | aren't they | did we | did you | do you | don't we | don't you | will he | won't he |

Ex.   *Those aren't your daughters,* ......*are they?*......

1   You don't all want to come on the hike, ...

2   He won't know about the change of plan, ...

3   The children are having lots of fun in the playground, ...

4   John will explain how to download those programs, ...

5   We didn't forget anything, ...

6   You speak English with a French accent, ...

7   You didn't see the burglar as he was running away, ...

8   We always order too much food when we come here, ...

5 ▶ Complete the sentences with a tag question.

Ex.   *She isn't the assistant that usually works here,* ....*is she?*............

1   You're interested in setting up your own business, ...

2   Everyone enjoyed themselves at the festival, ...

3   These aren't your car keys, ...

4   I've upset you, ...

5   You had never met him before you came here this evening, ...

6   Nobody has seen my jeans, ...

7   Ours will be the best wedding in the world, ...

8   Let's start planning the next project, ...

9   Don't forget that we're going out tonight, ...

10   He hardly ever takes part in discussions, ...

Thinkaboutit

Don't just look at the verb to decide if a sentence is affirmative or negative. Pay attention to words like **seldom, hardly ever, never, nobody,** etc.

Negative Questions

Negative questions are formed using the short form of *not (n't)*.

auxiliary + *n't* + subject + verb
Didn't you like the meal?

We use negative questions in everyday speech:

➤ when we want to confirm something.
Didn't he stay until the end of the play?

➤ to express surprise or amazement.
Don't you enjoy English?

➤ to show something is bothering us.
Can't you stop talking for five minutes?

6 ▶ **Choose the correct word.**

Ex. (Don't) / Aren't *you like going for long walks in the country?*

1 *Aren't / Won't* you the woman whose house we bought?
2 *Don't / Can't* you decide which hotel to stay at in London?
3 *Hasn't / Doesn't* she finished typing the report yet?
4 *Can't / Do* you stop leaving all your dirty clothes on the bathroom floor?
5 *Don't / Didn't* they say when they would be back from their vacation?
6 *Isn't / Doesn't* he just the kindest man you've ever met?
7 *Don't / Doesn't* the public library allow everyone to use its facilities?
8 *Don't / Couldn't* you go somewhere else to make all that noise?

7 ▶ **Match.**

Ex. *Don't you*   a notice his car was missing?
1 Wasn't he   b understand that I don't want them to come here again?
2 Can't they   c the man who had been accused of stealing cars?
3 Doesn't she   d *live somewhere on the other side of town?*
4 Aren't you   e want to move out of the apartment she's living in now?
5 Didn't he   f lose her job if she continues to take so much time off?
6 Won't she   g the woman who owns the flower shop on Main Street?

8 ▶ **Choose the correct word.**

Dan: Hi, Nina. I haven't seen you for ages. (Ex.) .... have you been doing?
Nina: Oh. Hi, Dan. Well, I've been working at home a lot, to be honest. (1) .... about you? (2) ....
        you ever manage to finish that project you were working on when I last saw you?
Dan: (3) .... project are you talking about?
Nina: The one you were asked to do by your boss, Mrs. Walters.
Dan: (4) .... you mean Mrs. Waters? Yes, I finished that. I'm working on a different project now.
Nina: (5) .... this one for?
Dan: It's for a sports equipment company in Chicago.
Nina: That means you might have to move there, (6) ....?
Dan: It's certainly a possibility.
Nina: In that case, (7) .... go out for dinner soon, shall we? Otherwise, I might not see you before you leave!
Dan: Good idea. (8) .... you busy this evening?
Nina: As it happens, I'm not. Let's make it this evening.
Dan: Right. (9) .... I pick you up at about 9 o'clock?
Nina: Sounds great. See you later.

Ex. (a) *What*   **b** *Which*   **c** *Where*

1 **a** Who   **b** Which   **c** What
2 **a** Do   **b** Did   **c** Have
3 **a** Where   **b** Which   **c** Who
4 **a** Can't   **b** Aren't   **c** Don't
5 **a** Who's   **b** Which is   **c** Whose
6 **a** isn't it   **b** won't it   **c** doesn't it
7 **a** do   **b** will   **c** let's
8 **a** Do   **b** Are   **c** Be
9 **a** Will   **b** Do   **c** Shall

9 ▶ **Find the extra word in each sentence and write it on the dotted line.**

Ex. *Do you know who this meal was it prepared by?* ....*it*.........

1   Judy is married to Richard, isn't she not? ....

2   Can't you not see that those jeans are too small for you? ....

3   Which car did he decide to buy it in the end? ....

4   She is not the most helpful person in the store, isn't she? ....

5   Don't you feel like staying in this evening and watching a little of TV? ....

6   Where have you put them the books I left on my desk? ....

7   Do you have an any idea where the Town Hall is? ....

8   Let's stop doing grammar exercises now, shall we do? ....

Pairwork

Work with a partner. Take turns pretending you are a famous person. Tell your partner who you are. Your partner will then interview you.

Writing

Imagine you have been asked by a magazine to interview one of the following:
➤ a famous athlete.
➤ a famous actor/actress.
➤ a famous pop star.
Choose which person you want to interview and then write the questions you are going to ask them when you meet.

SHE TURNED DOWN HIS OFFER OF A FRESH CUP OF COFFEE.

Phrasal Verbs – Get / Go

get away with – escape punishment
get back – return
get into – get inside a car, taxi, etc.
get on – make progress
get up – wake up and get out of bed

go off – explode with a loud noise (e.g., a bomb)
go off – start to ring (e.g., an alarm clock)
go on – continue
go out – stop burning or working (e.g., a fire, lights)
go up – rise, increase

He didn't get away with telling lies; they found
out the truth about him.
We must get back from lunch before two.
Get into the car and fasten your seat belt.
How are you getting on with your Spanish lessons?
He never gets up before seven.

We jumped when we heard a gun go off.
The burglar alarm went off for no reason.
The meeting will go on for another hour.
Why have the lights gone out?
The price of theater tickets has gone up by
five dollars.

---

1 ▷ **Complete the sentences with the correct particles.**

Ex.   Who gets .....*up*..... first in your house? You or another member of your family?

1   The police shouldn't let vandals get away .... damaging property.

2   Why have all the lights just gone ....?

3   Let's buy the new car now before prices go .... again.

4   We all had to evacuate the building when the fire alarm went ....

5   How are you getting .... in your new job?

6   If the garbage strike goes .... for much longer, the city will stink!

7   We didn't get .... the taxi because we didn't like the look of the driver!

8   If Jane gets .... before I do, please tell her that her dinner's ready.

2 ▶ Complete the sentences with the correct form of the phrasal verbs from the box.

| get away with | get back | get into | get up | go off (x2) | go on | go out | go up |

Ex.   We can't ....go on................ arguing every day like this.

1   I don't know why the burglar alarm ...., but I'm glad we knew how to stop it!
2   Why didn't you relight the fire when you realized it ....?
3   We took off our muddy shoes as soon as we .... the house.
4   No one .... cheating in Mr. Allen's class.
5   How much has the price of butter .... this year?
6   I have to .... before 6 o'clock tomorrow morning.
7   The starter's pistol .... with a loud bang, and the runners sprang into action!
8   I hope to .... before it gets dark.

Phrasal Verbs – Look / Put

look after – take care of
look for – search
look forward to – await with pleasure
look into – investigate
look out – be careful

Will you look after the cats while I'm away?
Can you help me look for my scarf?
I'm looking forward to seeing you again.
They are looking into the cause of the fire.
Look out! You almost ran over that dog!

put away – place something where it belongs
put off – delay
put on – get dressed in
put through – connect on the phone
put up – accommodate

Would you put the milk away for me?
I never put things off unless I have to.
Put on your heavy coat. It's freezing outside!
Can you put me through to Mr. Rivera's office, please?
He said he would put me up for a few days.

3 ▶ Choose the correct answer.

My best friend and I have just moved into a new apartment. So far we have had several arguments! For one thing, she doesn't put anything (Ex.) .... in the right place. She always says she is going to do it later, but I tell her she shouldn't keep (1) .... it off; she should do jobs like that right away. Another thing that annoys me is when she turns all the lights on and leaves them on all the time, even when she doesn't need them. The cost of electricity has gone (2) .... and our bills will get higher and higher if she (3) .... on like this. Luckily, the power went (4) .... yesterday, so that saved us some money! At first she used to do lots of jobs around the house, but now she tries to (5) .... doing as little as possible. Anyway, I hate to go (6) .... complaining about her, especially since her grandfather is sick and she has to go and look (7) .... him for a few weeks. To be honest, I'm looking (8) .... to having some time in the apartment without her.

Ex.   **a** *up*   **b** *off*   **(c)** *away*

1   **a** looking   **b** putting   **c** going
2   **a** off   **b** on   **c** up
3   **a** goes   **b** puts   **c** looks
4   **a** on   **b** out   **c** into
5   **a** get up   **b** put off   **c** get away with
6   **a** on   **b** off   **c** up
7   **a** for   **b** into   **c** after
8   **a** after   **b** forward   **c** into

4 ▶ **Match.**

Ex. *look after*   a   accommodate
1   put up   b   connect by phone
2   put off   c   dress in
3   look out   d   beware
4   look for   e   store in the correct place
5   put on   f   investigate
6   put away   g   delay
7   look into   h   *take care of*
8   put through   i   try to find

Phrasal Verbs – Take / Turn

take after – be like
take in – understand
take off – go up into the sky
take off – remove (e.g., clothing)
take out – escort or go out with

take up – start a hobby
turn down – refuse
turn off – switch off (e.g., a machine or light)
turn on – switch on (e.g., a machine or light)
turn out – happen in the end

Who do you take after in your family?
I couldn't take in anything she said.
Our flight takes off soon.
Why don't you take your coat off?
The children wish their parents would take them out more often.

Have you ever thought of taking up golf?
It was such a good offer I couldn't turn it down.
Turn off the lights before you leave, please.
Can I turn the heating on?
It's turned out to be a nice day after all.

---

5 ▶ **Complete the sentences with the correct form of the phrasal verbs from the box.**

| not take off | take in | take off | take up | turn down | turn off | turn out |

Ex. *Are you sure the plane* ....*doesn't take off*...... *until 10 a.m.?*

1   If you .... the radio ...., I would be able to hear you.

2   Good luck! I hope everything .... well for you.

3   You ought to .... a more energetic hobby like jogging.

4   No matter how many times I read the grammar rules, I just can't .... them ....

5   Mark asked Maria to marry him, but, amazingly, she .... him ....!

6   .... those dirty clothes and put them straight into the washing machine.

---

6 ▶ **Find the extra word in each sentence and write it on the dotted line.**

Ex. *Would you turn it off the radio, please?* ....*it*........

1   In the end, it will all turned out for the best. ....

2   I've told him how to do this ten times, but he hasn't done taken anything in. ....

3   We'd better turn on the outside lights off so the guests can see their way down the path. ....

4   He's has turned down a promotion twice, just so he doesn't have to do more work! ....

5   Did the plane take out off on time? ....

6   He doesn't seem to take him after either of his parents. ....

Verbs + Prepositions – About / From

complain about – say you are unhappy about
dream about – think about while asleep
hear about – be told about
think about – consider
warn (sb) about – tell of dangers or risks

borrow (sth) from (sb) – take (sth) temporarily
differ from – be different from
escape from – get away from
prevent (sb/sth) from – stop sb/sth from doing (sth)
return from – get back from

She always complains about her boss.
*Last night the secretary dreamed about having a
computer that types by itself.*
Did you hear about the murder in this area?
Why don't you think about a change of career?
Nobody warned me about the mosquitoes here!

He borrowed money from me last week.
I differ from my best friend in almost every way.
The prisoner escaped from a high-security prison.
I can't prevent my son from seeing his friends.
*They returned from their vacation only to find that their
house had been broken into.*

---

7 **Choose the correct answer.**

Ex.   *I often* dream */ hear about new houses. What do you think it means?*

1   I've *thought / complained* seriously about your offer, but I'm afraid I can't accept it.

2   What exactly is it that *differs / prevents* you from being happy here?

3   When are they expected to *return / borrow* from their trip?

4   I didn't *think / hear* about the accident until the police called to tell me.

5   He's always *hearing / complaining* about one thing or another.

6   Is it true that no prisoner ever *borrowed / escaped* from Alcatraz?

7   I didn't have anything to wear, so I *thought / borrowed* something from my cousin.

8   I *warned / complained* him about the dangers of smoking.

---

8 **Complete the sentences with the verbs from the box and a preposition.**

borrow	complain	differ	dream	escape	hear	prevent	return	think

Ex.   *We didn't* ......*hear about*...... *their wedding until the week before it took place.*

1   What do you .... when you're trying to fall asleep?

2   How can I .... Jamie .... biting his nails?

3   We .... each other when it comes to our ideas about bringing up children.

4   Maybe we ought to .... all the noise our neighbors make.

5   For some reason, I always .... strange things whenever I stay overnight at your house.

6   You can .... some money .... me if you promise to pay me back soon.

7   He can't wait to go to college so he can .... his three sisters!

8   When will the boss .... his trip to Brazil?

Verbs + Prepositions – For / Of

apologize for – say one is sorry for
arrest (sb) for – take into custody for
ask for – request
blame (sb) for – hold (sb) responsible for
wait for – remain until (sb) comes/(sth) happens

She apologized for the delay.
The police arrested him for car theft.
*I asked for directions, but nobody knew where
the place was.*
Don't blame me for your own carelessness!
What are you waiting for?

accuse (sb) of – say (sb) did (sth)
approve of – consider acceptable
consist of – be made up of
die of – stop living because of
rob (sb) of (sth) – steal (sth) from (sb)

He was accused of stealing money from the company.
I don't approve of people who hunt.
What exactly does this dish consist of?
She almost died of pneumonia.
They robbed the old lady of her life savings.

9 ▸ **Complete the sentences with for or of.**

Ex.   *My grandmother died ....of....... pneumonia at the age of ninety-nine.*

1   I must apologize .... not having written to you sooner.

2   I always get the blame .... things I didn't do!

3   Why are you accusing me .... lying to you?

4   How many times do I have to ask you .... my CDs back?

5   Which train are you waiting ....?

6   The boss approved .... our idea for the new ad campaign.

7   What exactly does this cake consist ....?

8   They ought to be arrested .... drawing all that graffiti in town!

Verbs + Prepositions – On / To

concentrate on – study or think about with care
congratulate (sb) on – give praise to (sb) for achieving (sth)
depend on – rely on
insist on – say sth must happen or be done
spend (money/time) on – pay for or be occupied with something

*If you don't concentrate on what he says, you won't understand
the problem.*
He congratulated me on winning the prize.
I depend on them for lots of things.
He insists on paying for everything.
He spends a lot of time on his hobbies.

apologize to (sb) – say you're sorry to (sb)
belong to – be owned by
complain to (sb) – show dissatisfaction to (sb)
object to – express displeasure with
point to – indicate with your finger

Why haven't you apologized to me?
Who does this bag belong to?
You should complain to the manager about the service
*Do you object to people using cell phones in
restaurants?*
Can you point to the person you think stole your bag?

> **Complete the sentences with the words from the box.**

| belonged | congratulate | insisted | object | on (x2) | pointing | to (x2) |

I can't understand why you ....object............ to staying at home on Sunday night.

Whether or not I get the job depends .... how well I do at the interview.

I didn't realize that house .... to your relatives.

It must have been difficult for you to apologize .... your brother.

I can't imagine spending so much money .... a pair of jeans.

I need to know who to complain .... about the poor service here.

Our boss .... on taking us all out to lunch on the last day of the month.

Can you see what that man is .... to?

I'd like to .... you on passing your driving test.

airwork

Work with a partner. Using the phrasal verbs and the verbs + prepositions you have learned in this unit, make up a story together. For example:

Student A: *Billy's aunt is always complaining about his clothes.*
Student B: *Billy's aunt is always complaining about his clothes. She insists on buying him old-fashioned things to wear.*
Student A: *Billy's aunt is always .... etc.*

riting

Write a short story about one of the following:
➤ an exciting adventure.
➤ a scary weekend.
➤ a hike in the mountains.

Try to use as many phrasal verbs and verbs + prepositions as you can.

....
....
....
....
....
....
....
....
....
....
....
....
....

1 ▸ Choose the correct answer.

Ex. *He really .... to have worked harder.*

    (**a**) *ought*   **b** *should*   **c** *shall*

1 You should .... been more polite to him.

    a has   **b** have   **c** ought

2 .... you stay for lunch?

    a Should   **b** Will   **c** Shall

3 .... I make us both a cup of coffee?

    a Shall   **b** Might   **c** Ought

4 I think he ought .... asking her out.

    a stop   **b** have stopped   **c** to stop

5 They .... have stolen the apples off that tree.

    a oughtn't   **b** shall   **c** shouldn't

6 Could I .... your new CD this evening, please?

    a to borrow   **b** borrow   **c** have borrow

7 You .... to get out more often.

    a could   **b** should   **c** ought

8 .... I make the dessert for supper tomorrow?

    a Ought   **b** Could   **c** Should be

2 ▸ Find the extra word.

Ex. *Could I be take you out tonight?* .... *be* ....

1 I should and make more of an effort to help around the house. ....

2 Those boys ought to not learn better manners! They're being very rude. ....

3 Can we have call and order a pizza for dinner? ....

4 Shall I can copy your notes onto the computer you? ....

5 Bearing in mind how ill he is, he really should consider it staying home this week. ....

6 I think you should ought to get a haircut! ....

7 I know! I'll shall go and buy us both some cake cheer us up! ....

8 He should to be more considerate of his friends family. ....

3 ▸ Rewrite the sentences using the words given. Use between two and five words.

Ex. *I'd be happy to help you move this weekend.* **can**

    I .... can help you move .... this weekend.

1 My children shouldn't waste so much money on computer games. **less**

    My children .... money on computer games.

2 They shouldn't have spoken so rudely to her. **ought**

    They .... more politely to her.

3 It was wrong of me not to practice the piano more regularly. **should**

    I .... more regularly.

4 Let's go to the beach today. **we**

    .... to the beach today?

5 The police are wrong not to investigate the robbery further. **should**

    The police .... the robbery further.

6 How about making new curtains for your bedroom? **could**

    You .... for your bedroom.

Complete the sentences using the past participle of the verbs from the box.

| check | grade | increase | pay for | prescribe | repair | send | service | upgrade |

He hasn't had his car .... *serviced* .... *for eighteen months.*

I had my passport .... to me through the mail.
The students will have their assignments .... by the head of the department.
We are going to have our computers .... by an expert.
The soldiers have their eyesight .... regularly.
The workers will have their pay .... by 5%.
I have had these vitamins .... for me by my doctor.
The football team will have their new uniforms .... by donations from local businesses.
We have been having our roof .... by a roofing company.

Complete the sentences using causative form.

The doctor took Tom's blood pressure.
Tom ..*had his blood pressure taken (by the doctor)..*

The nurse had taken my temperature.
I ....
....

The doctor will examine his chest.
He ....
....

The surgeon is taking out Jim's appendix.
Jim ....
....

4   The doctor was listening to her breathing.
    She ....
    ....

5   The assistant has X-rayed her lungs.
    She ....
    ....

6   The doctor gave her the X-ray results.
    She ....
    ....

Choose the correct answer.

They .... *an extension built onto their house at the moment.*
a had   **(b)** are having   **c** will have

I .... my health insurance paid for by my company.
a did have   **b** have   **c** am having

Mark .... his hair cut by the local barber, but now he goes into town.
a has   **b** used to have   **c** having

In our area we .... pizzas and Indian meals delivered.
a are having   **b** can have   **c** did have

Bill .... the tires on his car changed tomorrow.
a has   **b** is having   **c** had

When are you .... that coat cleaned?
a will have   **b** had   **c** going to have

At this time tomorrow I .... my hearing tested.
a having   **b** will have   **c** will be having

.... her new glasses made before she went on vacation?
a Has she had   **b** Did she had   **c** Had she had

We .... our lunch made for us yesterday by the new cook.
a are having   **b** had   **c** will had

7 Complete each question with one word.

Ex. *Do you have any* ....*idea*........ *how much they paid for their new house?*

1 Can you .... me where the bank is?
2 How .... has he been playing the drums?
3 .... is he going to call me back?
4 .... bus goes down Fifth Avenue?
5 .... was the living room painted by?
6 Could you tell me .... to get to the police station?
7 When .... you clean the kitchen?
8 Do you know .... the movie starts at 8:00 or 8:30?

8 Choose the correct answer.

Ex. *Don't / Can't you feel like going out tonight?*

1 *Who / Which* was that woman I saw you with last night?
2 *Isn't / Aren't* you the student who won the prize for the best composition of the year?
3 Do you have any *thought / idea* how far it is from Los Angeles to San Francisco?
4 *Don't / Can't* you do something useful for a change?
5 *Don't / Won't* you want to join the tennis club?
6 He had a good seat at the concert, *didn't / hadn't* he?
7 You *don't / didn't* live with your parents anymore, do you?
8 Do you *know / tell* where I can go to study Japanese?

9 Complete the questions with tag questions.

Ex. *This isn't the table we sat at last time,* ....*is it?*............

1 They've never been to China, ...
2 You won't forget the meeting tomorrow, ...
3 She was the girl you really wanted to marry, ...
4 I'm the greatest cook in the world, ...
5 You had written your report before the boss arrived at the office, ...
6 Let's play tennis tomorrow, ...
7 Today is Thursday, ...
8 Everyone has a notebook with them, ...

10 Complete the sentences with the correct particle.

Ex. *I would be able to see better if you turned* ....*on*............ *the lights in here.*

1 The professor is looking .... how the test papers could have been stolen from his office.
2 Jenny seems to be getting .... much better at work now that she has a new boss.
3 I'm hoping my aunt will be able to put me .... for a week while I'm in Chicago.
4 Did he really think he would get .... with lying to his parents?
5 Make sure Bobby brushes his teeth when he gets ....
6 You're not going out until you've put all your clothes and games ....
7 He set his alarm clock to go .... at 6:30 a.m.
8 The plane couldn't take .... because of the bad weather.

Choose the correct answer.

You can't .... anyone but yourself for your problems.

a accuse   **(b)** blame   **c** complain

My boss objected .... my idea of having a long lunch.

a for   **b** of   **c** to

I'm so glad I've got a friend like you who I can .... on.

a complain   **b** depend   **c** belong

Our apartment .... of five rooms.

a consists   **b** belongs   **c** points

Do you approve .... people who use their cell phones on buses?

a for   **b** to   **c** of

What was the teenager arrested ....?

a for   **b** of   **c** on

Her pet cat died .... a rare blood disease.

a for   **b** of   **c** to

We've sent you this card to congratulate you .... your promotion.

a on   **b** at   **c** to

Some parents .... on their children coming home before dark.

a complain   **b** wait   **c** insist

Rewrite the sentences correctly.

He looks after both his parents in different ways, but he's more like his father overall.
He takes after both his parents in different ways, but he's more like his father overall.

I had to complain to the fact that the food was cold.

Can you put me up to Customer Service, please?

We apologized to having left our books at home.

I was warned for the storm but I didn't think it would really happen.

He was robbed by his watch on a crowded bus.

Can you really concentrate to your reading when I'm playing loud music?

You spend a lot of money about shoes, don't you?

His busy schedule prevents him for going to the gym.

Irregular Verbs

Infinitive	Simple Past	Past Participle	Infinitive	Simple Past	Past Participle
be	was/were	been	lend	lent	lent
beat	beat	beaten	let	let	let
become	became	become	lie	lay	lain
begin	began	begun	light	lit	lit
bet	bet	bet	lose	lost	lost
bite	bit	bitten	make	made	made
bleed	bled	bled	mean	meant	meant
blow	blew	blown	meet	met	met
break	broke	broken	mistake	mistook	mistaken
bring	brought	brought	pay	paid	paid
build	built	built	put	put	put
burst	burst	burst	read	read	read
buy	bought	bought	ride	rode	ridden
catch	caught	caught	ring	rang	rung
choose	chose	chosen	rise	rose	risen
come	came	come	run	ran	run
cost	cost	cost	say	said	said
cut	cut	cut	see	saw	seen
deal	dealt	dealt	sell	sold	sold
dig	dug	dug	send	sent	sent
do	did	done	set	set	set
draw	drew	drawn	shake	shook	shaken
drink	drank	drunk	shine	shone	shone
drive	drove	driven	shoot	shot	shot
eat	ate	eaten	show	showed	shown
fall	fell	fallen	shut	shut	shut
feed	fed	fed	sing	sang	sung
feel	felt	felt	sit	sat	sat
fight	fought	fought	sleep	slept	slept
find	found	found	speak	spoke	spoken
fly	flew	flown	spend	spent	spent
forbid	forbade	forbidden	spread	spread	spread
forget	forgot	forgotten	spring	sprang	sprung
forgive	forgave	forgiven	stand	stood	stood
freeze	froze	frozen	steal	stole	stolen
get	got	got / gotten	stick	stuck	stuck
give	gave	given	sting	stung	stung
go	went	gone	sweep	swept	swept
grow	grew	grown	swim	swam	swum
have	had	had	take	took	taken
hear	heard	heard	teach	taught	taught
hide	hid	hidden	tell	told	told
hit	hit	hit	think	thought	thought
hold	held	held	throw	threw	thrown
hurt	hurt	hurt	understand	understood	understood
keep	kept	kept	wake	woke	woken
know	knew	known	wear	wore	worn
lay	laid	laid	win	won	won
lead	led	led	write	wrote	written
leave	left	left			

Notes

Notes